Taking God on Patrol

28 Years in Law Enforcement

MARK S. CARONNA

Copyright © 2014 Mark S. Caronna.

All rights reserved. No part of this book may be used or reproduced by any means, graphic, electronic, or mechanical, including photocopying, recording, taping or by any information storage retrieval system without the written permission of the publisher except in the case of brief quotations embodied in critical articles and reviews.

"Scripture taken from the New King James Version®. Copyright © 1982 by Thomas Nelson, Inc. Used by permission. All rights reserved."

"Scripture taken from the NEW AMERICAN STANDARD BIBLE®, Copyright © 1960,1962,1963,1968,1971,1972,1973,1975,1977 ,1995 by The Lockman Foundation. Used by permission."

WestBow Press books may be ordered through booksellers or by contacting:

WestBow Press
A Division of Thomas Nelson & Zondervan
1663 Liberty Drive
Bloomington, IN 47403
www.westbowpress.com
1 (866) 928-1240

Because of the dynamic nature of the Internet, any web addresses or links contained in this book may have changed since publication and may no longer be valid. The views expressed in this work are solely those of the author and do not necessarily reflect the views of the publisher, and the publisher hereby disclaims any responsibility for them.

Any people depicted in stock imagery provided by Thinkstock are models, and such images are being used for illustrative purposes only. Certain stock imagery © Thinkstock.

ISBN: 978-1-4908-2699-8 (sc)
ISBN: 978-1-4908-2700-1 (hc)
ISBN: 978-1-4908-2698-1 (e)

Library of Congress Control Number: 2014903538

Printed in the United States of America.

WestBow Press rev. date: 02/28/2014

Contents

Foreword vii

Introduction ix

1. Knights in Armor 1
2. Shots Fired 5
3. Purpose of Heart 10
4. The Test of Faith 15
5. DOA 23
6. Mr. Roy Hand 28
7. Slow Days at Beechnut 32
8. Rookies 38
9. Ponderosa and the Chase 45
10. Where's the Fire? 57
11. Caught Red-Handed 63
12. Dealing with Death 72
13. Shine Your Light 77
14. Sixteen Days in July 84

15. Danger and Overconfidence 91
16. The Welfare Check 102
17. Compassion 109
18. Bear One Another's Burdens 115
19. The Devil Is Real 124
20. Who Will Stand Up? 129
21. Without Natural Affection 136
22. Taking Chances 142
23. Wrap-Up 153

Foreword

Taking God on Patrol is a unique look at the practical side of law enforcement through the lens of a Christian who, without jettisoning his own faith and principles, connects the dots between the sometimes elusive and contradicting nexus of authority, oath, values, teamwork, duty, and ethics. It is a matter-of-fact recounting of real-life events as they unfolded in the daily interactions between the people and the police. In penning his stories, which cover nearly three decades of experience, Mark bucks the often-cited *Code of Silence* used to describe the willful blindness and deliberate indifference of wrongdoing by those who donned the badge and swore to serve the people. But his stories also speak to those moments and times of decision-making that face all of us. Whether the call involves a death investigation or a welfare check, Mark brings the circumstances to life. In doing so, the reader gets a front seat ride-along with him as he receives, answers, and responds to a variety of problems and calls for assistance.

I recommend this book for those looking to pursue a law enforcement career, wanting to study ethical dilemmas in policing, or trying to preserve and uphold their own faith in a secular world of rules and rubrics. I also recommend it for those who never considered themselves religious or necessarily heeded that still-small voice that resonates within our hearts. Whether you never read the Bible or read it regularly, Mark denotes the biblical passages that enlighten and empower a person to deal with the circumstances presented. And, after all, it is not our circumstances that define us; but how we respond to them surely will.

Dwayne Ready
Captain, Homicide Division
Houston Police Department

Introduction

The career of a law enforcement officer is at one moment terribly boring and routine, and the next terribly frightening and deadly. Fortunately, some of the things an officer encounters are terribly funny as well.

Many of us joined the force because we had watched television programs that glamorized police work, made it seem exciting, or showed how helpful and loved police officers were. Yeah, sure.

Rarely does anyone call the police and say, "Officer, how are you doing today? I just wanted you to come by and share a meal with me" or "Officer, tell me how you like your job." Officers meet people in crisis, at the worst moments of their lives, and occasionally at the end of their lives. Many times a police officer is the last person anyone wants to see, and the last person some ever do see.

The situations that those of us on the job find ourselves in can and will test our faith, friendships, family, and marriage relationships. Nothing currently shown on television truly depicts the realities of the difficulty, horror, sadness, and even humorous things a law enforcement officer experiences on a regular basis.

You may not be employed in law enforcement, but you too experience a wide array of sights, sounds, and emotions during your day. If you are a Christian, then remember that you are representing Jesus in a landscape that is broken, scarred, and engaged in a spiritual war every day. Be certain that you are not leaving God behind when you show up for duty each day.

This book is an account of just a few of the things I encountered during twenty-eight years as one of Houston's finest, and the lessons that I learned from them. Names and dates have been changed, but the situations were very real. This is not a children's book. I pray that you will find something here to strengthen your faith, and to challenge, encourage, or teach you as we take God on patrol.

1

KNIGHTS IN ARMOR

I grew up in Southwest Houston in the Meyerland area in the 1960s. My family was close-knit, as most Sicilian immigrant families were. When asked why I chose to be a cop—as many of my friends and acquaintances made their fortunes in the oil field or, more recently, in computers—I must go back to my early days and my first chance to see an officer up close in order to answer that question.

My parents had four children, and I was the youngest. I was around six or seven years old when an incident occurred that would catch my attention and direct my life. One evening after my father had arrived home from work, I was doing what I did best: playing. While happily occupied with G.I. Joe, I heard a woman scream outside our home. My father ran past me toward the front door, telling us to get away from the windows as he looked outside. Taking action must run in the family. Dad disappeared down the hall, quickly returning with a small, .380 semiautomatic pistol in his hand. Dad was immediately on the phone, calling the police to report the woman's screams and providing the three Ds: details, directions, and descriptions. In short order, the police arrived.

Now, this is not necessarily going to make the evening news, but what happened next would change my life forever. It was something I would find myself doing many times in the years to come. The police arrived and entered our home to speak with my father. There they were. To my young eyes, they looked like they were nine feet tall. They were dressed in their blue uniforms—sharp, clean, and professional. The gold lettering on their shoulder patches seemed to glow, matched only by the shine of their silver badges, shiny shoes, and flap holsters. To me, these officers were in the top three on my list of the all-time greatest men living—right behind my dad, and of course, God Himself. These men were like knights in King Arthur's court—noble, strong, fearless, and honest. I knew then that someday, in some way, I had to be like them, to be one of them. They were there to help, and I wanted to do the same.

Some years later, in April 1983, I graduated Cadet Class 110. I felt both fearless and fearful at the same time. What if I could not live up to the standard, the calling of God to be a police officer, a peace officer?

People enter the job market every day, and many give little thought to their chosen fields. Some enter a particular field because it will make the most money, or perhaps because it is all they are qualified to do, or it's what their families expect them to do. Some enter a career field that they enjoy, regardless of the pay and benefits. I entered the field of law enforcement because I believed (and still do believe) that I accepted a call from God to help others.

Those of you who have made the same choice know it isn't the best-paying job, and you are often held in contempt or scorned by the very people you are sworn to protect. When we take the oath, we step out in front of society to lead, protect, and help. In John 15:13, Jesus said, "Greater love has no one than this, that one lay down his life for his friends." He also said, "And whoever wishes to be first among you shall be slave of all" (Mark 10:44 NASB). We know—or soon come to know—that our profession is about sacrifice and service, just as Jesus' life was. Over the years, those words have kept me going at times when I questioned my own sanity for even doing this job.

Why didn't I get a normal job with normal hours and responsibilities? I have to remember that I answered a call from our Lord, who came to serve, not to be served. So, rather than go it alone, I took my faith along. I took God on patrol. There were many struggles, times I doubted, times I failed, and times of victory during the twenty-eight years I served in law enforcement. Regardless of how you view your job, do it as unto the Lord. Do it to the best of your abilities, and never stop learning.

Shots Fired

The field training program is stressful for a rookie officer. In the 1980s, it consisted of three fifteen-day training cycles on all three shifts: days, evenings, and nights. The trainer had to cover every category listed in the training manual for the particular phase of training, and each phase built upon the accomplishments of the previous phase. After these initial training cycles came the dreaded evaluation phase: two weeks of pure, nervous misery spent riding with a field performance evaluator (FPE).

The FPE sits quietly in the passenger seat and pretends that he or she is not there. The rookie being evaluated must handle the entire shift from start to finish with no help from the FPE—unless death or serious bodily harm is imminent. Occasionally, the FPE will ask the rookie questions, making notes in a little spiral notebook throughout the eight-hour tour.

My evaluation phase took place in the southwest part of the city, in and around Houston's Sunnyside neighborhood. My FPE, Carl, seemed fair enough and was more laid-back than most. This was a good thing because up until this point, policing did not come naturally for me, and Carl's laid-back approach eased the stress I was under.

We were on the late side evening shift, when we received a disturbance call at a local drugstore on the corner of Scott Street and Mt. Pleasant. Interesting name, Mt. Pleasant—it kind of makes you feel at-ease and safe. This call would turn out to be anything but pleasant for us that evening.

We arrived without much difficulty, even with me behind the wheel, heading north on Scott Street. My focus was on the intersection of Scott and Mt. Pleasant. Luckily for us, I missed the location and drove past the drugstore. Had I driven directly to the location and stopped, our day might have ended tragically.

Bang! A shot rang out very close by. I turned to Carl, and he looked at me. Outside of our car, I noticed several firefighters sitting behind a fire station to the north. They were all pointing behind our car at a man who had just fired point-blank at Carl's window.

Carl grabbed the radio and shouted into the mic, "15E20, shots fired, we have shots fired!"

My heart immediately jumped into adrenaline overdrive. *Had someone just shot at us?* I wondered. Duh!

"Turn right!" Carl shouted.

I turned the car right at the corner, and we sped down the street, making another right at the next corner. We approached the corner drugstore from behind.

"Get your gun out," Carl said. That should have been a no-brainer, but I was a rookie, just twenty-two years old. As time went on, my sidearm came out of the holster often. It would become second nature.

Holding the steering wheel with one hand, I flipped open the flap holster with my other shaky hand. *Which direction do I point this gun? How am I going to drive with one hand? Maybe I can stick this between my legs so I can drive with two hands. No, bad idea, I might shoot myself in the—*

"Slow down. Get ready," came Carl's voice, jolting me back to the present situation.

My head swiveled as I tried to see out of the patrol car in every direction at once, my view hindered by the protective screen behind me. *Where is the bad guy who shot at us? Is he still there, waiting for us? How have I not seen him?*

We bailed out of the car, and surprisingly enough, no bad guy was around. In fact, nothing seemed to be out-of-the-ordinary on that corner at all. People were coming and going normally. The adrenaline that had just moments ago been at level twelve on a scale of one to ten, was now left flooding my bloodstream with nothing to do. It's amazing how tired you feel when that happens.

In a matter of minutes, the bad guy returned to that corner with a fresh change of clothes and an attempt to blend in with the crowd that had gathered. Someone pointed him out, and we arrested him, bagging his hands for a later test for gunpowder residue. He had been just a few yards away when he'd fired at us, but we could not find as much as a scratch on our car. How could he have missed?

And how could I keep the anger from rising up within me at this man who had moments before attempted to take our lives? Actually, the anger was already there, so the question became: would I control the anger? Could a Christian become that angry with someone and not sin? These emotions were a confusing struggle for me. I had been angry before, but never at someone who had, moments before, attempted to end my life.

Had God been with me on patrol that day? I know that He had. Psalm 91 soon became a precious promise to me. "He who dwells in the shelter of the Most High will abide in the shadow of the Almighty. I will say to the LORD, 'My refuge and my fortress, My God, in whom I trust!' For it is He who delivers you from the snare of the trapper and from the deadly pestilence. He will cover you with His pinions, and under His wings you may seek refuge; His faithfulness is a shield and bulwark" (Psalm 91:1–4 NASB).

I was (and am still) convinced that God was true to His Word that day—and has been every day since then. Later, I had a silver butt plate made that attached to the grip of my revolver. It read "Psalm 91," and over the years it became a key that opened doors to share my faith with many fellow officers. The shelter of God carries the idea of being a hiding or secret place. To abide there is to abide in Him. The unity and safety found by abiding in God does not mean that physical harm will never come to you but that you are spiritually protected in Him. Abide in God, find your rest in Him, and experience His protection, eternal life, and amazing love—no matter what happens on your patrol.

3

PURPOSE OF HEART

"But Daniel purposed in his heart that he would not defile himself with the portion of the king's delicacies, nor with the wine which he drank" (Daniel 1:8 NKJV).

What is it about being a Christian that makes it hard to be a cop? Maybe I have that question backward. What it is about being a cop that makes it hard to be a Christian? How do I love my enemies when they are literally trying to kill me? How do I show the love and compassion of Christ and still be tough enough to catch the crooks? How do I remain true to my convictions with the peer pressure that comes with the brotherhood of law enforcement's thin blue line? These questions were ever present early in my career.

Let's learn from Daniel. About 650 B.C. the king of Babylon, Nebuchadnezzar, was on a roll. He had defeated the armies of Assyria, Egypt, and now Jerusalem. King Nebuchadnezzar decided to take captive some of the best young men in Jerusalem.

They would be trained as servants in the king's courts. One of these young men was named Daniel.

Daniel had no choice but to go. However, he did have a choice as to how he would behave while in captivity. Daniel purposed in his heart not to be defiled. Now, what does that mean? For Daniel, to "purpose in his heart" meant that he had drawn a line in the sand, so to speak, past which he absolutely would not cross. The "heart" is the inner person and includes the mind, emotions, and will. Daniel had decided beforehand to remain true to God and to his own convictions, which were based upon God's Word, regardless of the consequences. Daniel didn't wait until he was in captivity to decide how he should conduct himself. He had decided long before to follow after God and be a godly man, but his captivity made that choice very real. The rewards of compromise are temporary and do not compare to the rewards of remaining faithful to the Lord.

Police officers take an oath of office the night they graduate from the training academy. Part of that oath is that we will uphold the US Constitution and the laws and ordinances of the state, county, and/or city. We figuratively draw a line in the sand with our words when we take that oath. Why, then, do so many officers find themselves compromised just a few short years down the road? Perhaps it is because they purposed in their *heads* to do those things rather than in their *hearts*. That is to say that a verbal acknowledgment alone of the terms and conditions of the oath of office—an acknowledgment that lacks an inner acceptance by the mind, emotions, and will—may very well end in failure. This is often what happens to marriages, when one or both partners fail to understand and accept the seriousness of the covenant they have entered into with God. Having an attitude that considers divorce an option if things don't "work out" sets one up to fail.

One day while I was in the training academy, an instructor made a shocking prediction. He said, "Within five years, 95 percent of you who are married will be divorced." Unfortunately, his prediction came true for many of my married classmates. Right then and there, I purposed in my heart not to be in the 95 percent group.

I was newly married and intended to remain so. Our first child would be born ten days before my graduation from the academy. My decision that day was a commitment to God. I had already entered into a covenant with God and my wife, and the instructor's prediction challenged my covenant. I simply could not allow that. Temptations to violate the covenant of marriage or the oaths of office abounded. Remember that God will never tempt you to violate your covenant or oath. James 1:13–14 tells us plainly that God never does that.

One night, years later, while I worked with a squad in the narcotics division, we ended up in Baytown, Texas, on a money-laundering case. I ended up transporting two suspects back to Houston to book them into the city jail. It was late and far past the end of my shift, and I was very tired. As was the routine then, I flipped up the removable rear seat of the patrol car to make certain that no contraband had been left behind for the next officer to find.

To my surprise, what did I find? I found ninety-two twenty-dollar bills, all wrapped up with a rubber band. Let's do the math here: 92 times 20 equals ... $1,840. Not a bad tip for the extra work that night, especially when a paycheck for two weeks in those days barely broke $700.00. Finders keepers, right? Wasn't this just God blessing me? After all, He knew that we struggled to make ends meet on a cop's salary. I mean, who would even know if I kept that money? It had belonged to a crook, and he was going to jail for a very long time, so he wouldn't miss it. Besides, I could tithe on it, right? Wouldn't that make God happy?

Regardless of all these well-thought-out arguments in favor of pocketing the money, I had purposed some things in my heart long ago—that I would remain honest, that I would remain true to the covenant I had made with God and my wife, and that I would become and remain a man of integrity. Nothing could move me away from my covenant with God. I could not see that money as a gift from God, though I gave it much thought. Our ethics should never be situational. They must be founded upon God's never-changing, never-compromising Word. Taking what does not belong to you is theft, plain and simple. Don't complicate the truth with well-thought-out justifications.

I spent a good amount of time locating the narcotics squad at breakfast. I walked into the restaurant and handed the money to the sergeant in charge and told him where I had found it. It was hard to decipher the look on his face. It seemed to range between, "Why didn't you just keep it?" and "Great, now I have more work to do, tagging it as evidence!" No matter, I had remained true to God and to myself. It was only a small victory, and it had not been as easy as it probably should have been. That night I refused to compromise. More difficult things awaited me.

THE TEST OF FAITH

"If you are reproached for the name of Christ, blessed are you, for the Spirit of glory and of God rests upon you. On their part He is blasphemed, but on your part He is glorified" (1 Peter 4:14 NKJV).

I graduated from police school in April 1983. I spent the weekend after graduation thinking and praying about Monday morning. Monday morning would take me to my patrol station, my first assignment. I didn't know what awaited me. I felt a sense of pride and relief for having survived cadet training, but to be honest, I was just a bit more than nervous about Monday morning. The station to which I had been assigned for the field-training program had a reputation for eating rookies alive. I had heard that no rookies made it through the evaluation phase successfully the first time through, and many didn't make it at all. Little did I know that I would face not only a difficult time on the job, but one of the toughest trials I would ever face as a Christian.

The gospels record that when Jesus was arrested, His disciples fled, and He was left alone to face ridicule, scorn, and eventual death. How lonely must Jesus have felt? He was simply obeying His Father, and for that He suffered so much. I was about to get a small taste of that in the years to come.

In the summer of 1983, I was a probationary police officer (PPO)—a rookie. I wouldn't be "real" police until after completing my first year, and then only if I passed the field-training program. In between training phases, or when one's training officer was away, rookies rode with another senior officer. For reasons unknown to me, this is called "floating."

One evening I was floating with a senior officer rumored to be a Christian. I was kind of looking forward to this shift, but being a rookie and easily intimidated, I wasn't sure how to strike up the conversation. We were riding in the old eighteenth district when a police pursuit was broadcast over the radio. For some reason, my senior partner didn't get involved in the chase, but he did go by the scene when the chase was declared to be over.

I recall vividly the excitement at being on the scene of a police chase for the first time. We walked forward from where we parked our patrol car to the front of the line of tow trucks and police cars from several different agencies. It was exciting to be a part of a real police scene. However, when I reached the spot where the suspects were, I stopped short. What I saw seemed to be taking place in slow motion. There were the three suspects, all handcuffed, all lying on the ground, and a number of police officers were beating and kicking them repeatedly. I looked from the officers and to the crowd of tow truck drivers and even to a fellow classmate. The look on my face must have read: *shock*.

I turned, somewhat dazed, and began to walk back toward our patrol car. Where was my partner? What was going on? Was I supposed to do something, to say something? I wanted to get away from what was happening. I didn't know much, but I knew enough to know that I didn't want to be a part of this scene. Still yards away, I could see through the windshield that my partner was already sitting in our patrol car. His white-knuckled hands gripped the steering wheel, for he was anxious to drive away. He signaled me to hurry up. I got in, and without any words being said, he began to drive quickly away from the scene. Neither of us said a word about the incident for the remainder of the day. In fact, I do not recall ever having a conversation of any kind with him after that day.

Months passed. I tried to forget about the whole incident, and I thought that I had. I was focused on passing the field-training program. But the issue wasn't going away. I had taken an oath; I had entered a covenant.

One afternoon, the phone rang in the patrol station. It was for me. The voice on the other end of the line sounded friendly enough. It was a sergeant from the Internal Affairs Division (IAD). He wanted to refresh my memory and asked me if I recalled the incident of the chase months earlier. The suspects had filed a brutality complaint against the officers involved in the incident, and I was instructed to come down and give a statement about what, if anything, I had seen. My heart stopped beating for a moment, and a cold chill ran up and down my entire body. Why was this happening now? I was a rookie with no civil service protection, and soon I would have no friends at the station.

The career death sentence for a rookie in 1983 was to be a labeled a "snitch." To be a snitch was to have betrayed the brotherhood of officers, to have crossed the line. There is an unhealthy "us versus them" mentality that often develops in law enforcement. To be a snitch was to be with "them." I so wanted to be accepted as one of the guys, to fit in, but I knew what I had to do. God demands honesty of His people, period—no discussion and no compromise.

Why was this happening to me? Was God punishing me? I was scared to death. I had nowhere to turn except to God Himself. Although I had no real friends there at the station, I knew that I was not alone, just as Jesus was not alone before the Sanhedrin or before Pontius Pilate.

Psalm 37:28 (NASB) says, "For the Lord loves justice, and does not forsake His godly ones; they are preserved forever, but the descendants of the wicked will be cut off." It didn't take long before the officers involved began to pressure me. I was just a rookie. They could easily make me lie about the incident—or so they thought. If they couldn't get me on their side, then they would do all they could to see that I did not succeed in training, that I would be terminated. Veteran officers whom I believed did not even know I existed suddenly wanted to befriend me. I showed up at IAD, and to my surprise, one of the accused officers was sitting there. We exchanged shallow greetings. He eyed me warily. I was the rookie, the unknown factor, unproven in battle and internal affairs investigations.

In the John 14:27 (NASB), Jesus promised to give peace: "Peace I leave with you; My peace I give to you; not as the world gives do I give to you. Do not let your heart be troubled, nor let it be fearful." I needed that peace right then and in a tangible way.

So, I did what was unthinkable in many police circles in the 1980s: I told the truth. Somehow I felt that God was pleased with me as I drove away. I had passed a test, a milestone in my Christian journey.

For more than three years, I endured hate mail, ridicule over the police radio, officers refusing to back me up on calls or blocking my radio transmissions, nasty things written about me on bathroom walls, and more. When I transferred to another patrol station in 1984, the persecution followed. I was paired up with another less-than-popular officer. When patrolling on the night shift, we were often followed, shadowed by officers in other patrol cars who were waiting for us to mess up to be reported to the station lieutenant—whom I found out later was determined to get rid of "the snitch." I was literally cursed to my face by supervisors, given the worst assignments, and generally hated. I was not trusted.

I began to feel less and less peace. I experienced loneliness deeper than I knew was possible. I wondered if this was how Jesus had felt when His disciples fled from Him in the garden of Gethsemane on the night of His arrest. This feeling was painful, but somewhere within me, I knew that God had not abandoned me. Loneliness is a strong motivator. Often it motivates people to compromise or to take drastic measures to alleviate its pain.

Was my honesty worth it? Wouldn't it have been better just to lie and say that I hadn't seen a thing? God would understand, wouldn't He? I mean, after all, Peter had lied about knowing Jesus and had even cursed about the very suggestion, yet he had been forgiven and used in a mighty way. The answer to my internal questions was a resounding *no*. God was always with me through all the trouble and loneliness. The pain was very real, but God demands honesty and justice.

True fellowship with Jesus is found when we share in His suffering. Paul indicates that in Philippians 3:10.

I discovered during this incident that no one, other than me, had told the truth—not even the senior officer known around the station as a Christian. Every other officer and witness, to a man, had chosen to lie. Why did they do that? I believe that the police culture of the day made it almost inevitable. I had chosen to obey my heavenly Father, and I suffered for it. I shed many tears and endured many sleepless nights following this incident, but it does not compare to the sufferings of Christ Jesus, who gave His life to save my soul. I do not pretend to be perfect in this or any other situation. Remember that I had first chosen to say nothing in hopes that it would all just go away. But God called me on my integrity and my profession of love for Him. Today my police ID reads, "Honorably Retired." The suffering of those years does not compare with the satisfaction of knowing that I made it successfully through the difficulties and loneliness. I believe that you can make it through as well.

Each individual must decide what to do when the tough situations come. If you want to do right, then you absolutely cannot wait until the test comes to you. You must make your decision before the test arrives. You must already have drawn the line in the sand across which you will not step, no matter what. You must have purposed in your heart not to be defiled by anything, not even popularity or acceptance by a social group.

Christian, you don't have to go along with the crowd to survive. In fact, you will not survive for long that way. As a Christian you will never fully be a part of the "in" crowd of the world, and you shouldn't desire to be. Additionally, when you stand upon God's Word without compromise, you will at times find yourself outside of even some church circles.

What trials are you facing today? What lies before you that you want so desperately to avoid? Is there something that you want to just go away, but it keeps coming back up before you? I encourage you to submit yourself to the Lord and stand upon His Word. He is faithful!

DOA

DOA means "dead on arrival." It's a term that police officers become very familiar with. Someone, somewhere, has passed from this life into the next. Unless the Lord returns, we all will die someday and spend an eternity somewhere. This appointment we cannot avoid, and we will not be late arriving for it.

It was another hot Houston evening. I was still patrolling in Southwest Houston and was about to encounter my first shooting call. With directions given by my trainer, I drove to the location. It was a nice brick home in a nice neighborhood. The story was that a woman had arrived home from the grocery store, her arms filled with bags, and entered her home to be confronted by an armed burglar. Without hesitation, the intruder had shot the woman. She fled as far as her garage before she fell and died. This was where we found her upon our arrival on scene.

Now, let me stop for a moment to say that a burglar is a coward and a thief. A burglar, like the Devil himself, has only one thing on his mind: to steal what is not his. For some reason, this burglar decided to take an innocent life on that hot afternoon and changed from cowardly thief to cowardly murderer.

I had been to funerals before. My grandparents had lived long, productive lives and had died of natural causes. However, I was now filled with strange emotions unfamiliar to me, a mixture of sorrow and anger. This woman had simply been taking care of her family when her life was tragically ended. This seemed so unfair to me, and I questioned God about it. Does God get angry over murder, violence, or other unjust and wrong acts? Was Abel, the first murder victim in history, doing anything wrong that day in the field when his brother, Cain, murdered him? Just like this woman, Abel's death had been undeserved, unnecessary, and unprovoked.

"Then the LORD said to Cain, 'Where is Abel your brother?' And he said, 'I do not know. Am I my brother's keeper?' He said, 'What have you done? The voice of your brother's blood is crying to Me from the ground. Now you are cursed from the ground, which has opened its mouth to receive your brother's blood from your hand" (Genesis 4:9–11 NASB).

You may be asking, "What does that have to do with me? I've never murdered anyone." Perhaps not—hopefully not—but Scripture gives us stern warnings about even our attitudes and feelings about our brothers in 1 John 3:15.

I stood on the southern bank of a wide drainage ditch that ran behind the murder victim's house, guarding evidence dropped by the crook as he fled the scene. While I stood there mulling over all of these things and melting under the hot sun, a neighbor of the woman came by to see what had happened. He was shocked to learn of the death of his kind neighbor.

"What is this world coming to?" he asked.

Murder is nothing new. It wasn't new to Houston, Texas, nor to the neighborhood. But when it hits this close to home, it becomes real. It is no longer something in movies or television shows—or a tragedy that only happens to other people. In this situation, no one could change the channel to look for something wonderful or entertaining to divert their attention. As we stood there along the drainage ditch, I took advantage of the open door and shared Christ with the man.

> You have heard that it was said to those of old, "You shall not murder, and whoever murders will be in danger of the judgment." But I say to you that whoever is angry with his brother without a cause shall be in danger of the judgment. And whoever says to his brother, "Raca!" shall be in danger of the council. But whoever says, "You fool!" shall be in danger of hell fire. Therefore

> if you bring your gift to the altar, and there remember that your brother has something against you, leave your gift there before the altar, and go your way. First be reconciled to your brother, and then come and offer your gift. (Matthew 5:21–24 NKJV)

Likely, you have never committed a murder, nor ever will. However, we must understand just how God views our unrighteous anger and hurtful words.

Are you harboring anger in your heart today? Are you planning, plotting, and waiting for a chance to get even with someone? Maybe it is your spouse or your parents. Notice in the above verses from the gospel of Matthew that Jesus began a section of His sermon by talking about murder. From there, He moved directly into bitterness, anger, and disrespectful talk toward another person. Why? I believe it is because all unjustified, rash anger is murder within the heart. It's not just the physical act of ending an innocent person's physical life that God considers wrong.

Don't allow bitterness and anger to take root in your life. Unforgiveness, bitterness, and anger can destroy you, your marriage, or other relationships. Are you running away from God? Are you blaming God for something that has happened in your life? Are you angry with God because of some unfulfilled expectations or prayer?

Just as Jesus commands reconciliation with your brother, be reconciled to God today. Call on Him, pray to Him, confess to Him your feelings of bitterness and anger, and then forsake them. Go with God on patrol today with a clean heart.

6

Mr. Roy Hand

Have you ever taken notice of a homeless person and wondered what events in life led him or her to that point? Some, no doubt, ended up that way as a result of drug or alcohol abuse. Some find themselves there because of mental illness, failed business ventures, gambling their lives away, or years of abuse or abandonment. There is a myriad of reasons or root causes. I would be willing to bet, though, that no one begins life with the intention of growing up to become a homeless adult.

Of the hundreds of homeless men, women, and even children that I have met during my career, one homeless man remains firmly in my memory. His name was Roy Hand. What a cool name. The name alone conjures up images of a tough guy, a cowboy, or an otherwise manly man.

I met Roy when I answered a call one night regarding a suspicious male in Houston's Neartown.

Roy was a bit rough-looking. He had seen many years of hardship. How Roy had come to be the suspicious man on the street, I do not know. Roy told me that at one time in his life he had been a Golden Gloves boxer, and the scars on his face lent some credence to his claim. Roy had held jobs over the years—all labor-intensive, blue collar stuff. He had been self-sufficient and proud. Unfortunately for Roy, years of alcohol abuse had taken their toll. It had brought him to a point in life where he spent most of the night walking the lonely streets, talking to imaginary people. Roy seemed to be haunted by his past—as well as his present life situation.

One particular night, I received a call involving Roy. I arrived to find Roy sitting on a sidewalk, crying. I knelt beside him and asked what was wrong. Suddenly he began to scream and point. It caused me to jump back, almost right out of my skin.

"Get them away! Get them off of me!" Roy screamed. He flailed his arms wildly about, as if he was trying to swat something away.

"What, Roy?" I asked. "Get what away?"

"They're biting me. The horses—get the horses … aagh!"

The look on Roy's face told me that whatever it was that was after him was very real to him. I didn't see horses biting Roy, but he did. The terror was on his face and in his voice. A couple of other officers and some paramedics on the call seemed as shocked at Roy's outburst as I was.

I felt the tug of the Holy Spirit. I needed to offer some help to comfort Roy. We are taught in police school not to become involved in someone's psychotic episode but to remain calm and to reassure him. This time, it wasn't going to help Roy to calmly say, "Now, Mr. Hand, sir, there are no horses biting you. They are only a figment of your imagination. Now calm down, sir, and allow me to talk to you about your life issues."

The fear in Roy's voice and the real tears coming from his eyes defrosted the chill that had been creeping in upon my now-veteran policeman's heart. So, there on the sidewalk in front of my colleagues, I began chasing the horses away—actually yelling at them. Then, turning to Roy, I told him that I had chased the horses away and that he was safe now. I hoped that my bluff would work. I stayed on the sidewalk with Roy until an ambulance transported him to a local hospital.

I never saw Roy Hand after that incident, and what became of him, I do not know. If his story is like so many others', Roy got a good night's sleep and a warm meal before returning to the streets to run from the demons that chased him nightly. I genuinely wanted to help Roy, but I wasn't sure how to go about it. This may sound cold and uncaring, but Roy Hand—like many others in similar situations—was reaping what he had sown so many years ago. We will indeed reap what we sow. A pastor friend of mine has often said,

"You reap what you sow, later than you sowed it, and in more abundance than you sowed."

You and I are sowing seeds of some kind. Everyone is. We sow seeds into the lives of our families, into our marriages, and into the hearts of our children. Are you sowing seeds, even tiny ones, that will someday spring up to bring you harm—or peace and safety? "Do not be deceived, God is not mocked; for whatever a man sows, that he will also reap" (Galatians 6:7 NKJV).

Sometimes we may sow little flirtations that can, and sometimes do, spring up into adultery, destroying our marriage and our testimony. Many of my fellow officers have sowed little seeds of social drinking, and more than a few have reaped a harvest of alcoholism or a career- or life-ending incident. Maybe you are sowing seeds of complacency, failing to do what you know to be good. "Therefore, to one who knows the right thing to do and does not do it, to him it is sin" (James 4:17 NASB).

I hope you are sowing good seeds that will reap a harvest of God's blessings. Good seeds can include sharing your faith in Christ and offering comfort or assistance to someone in need.

You are always sowing seeds. What seeds are you sowing?

Slow Days at Beechnut

In 1983 I rode with an old department head, whom I will refer to as O.H., in a part of town that was new to me. I absolutely hated riding with this guy, and each day seemed to crawl. O.H. was ancient, and he seemed to be angry at everything and everyone, which was demonstrated by his constant cursing at everything and everyone, including me. "Why did you even take this job?" he once asked me. That question stuck with me, and I asked it of myself a number of times over the years. After only one week of patrolling with the guy, I seriously considered resigning from the department and returning to college.

It seemed that O.H. specialized in obtaining a free local newspaper each day and eating free doughnuts. He was king of "dragging the sack," which is slang for obtaining a free meal. This was once a common occurance for uniformed officers. I did learn one very important thing from him: how to drive the police car with one hand while not spilling the coffee I was holding in the other hand. This was a true police skill that would come in handy for years to come. When done well, one's coffee arm and hand became a sort of suspension system, like one of those air-cushioned seats on an eighteen-wheeler.

O.H. and I received a call from the juvenile division one morning. They had a kid in custody for the burglary of a local school, and they directed us to locate his accomplice, Michael. O.H. knew the area well, and he knew where to look for the accomplice. I was so glad that we were finally going to do some police work.

O.H. took us to all kinds of shady-looking establishments, places I would never have gone had I not been wearing the uniform and carrying a loaded sidearm. O.H. seemed to own these streets, and the people we encountered seemed to know that he meant business and that he was "The Man." I tried to walk the way he did, to command the respect he did, but it was obvious to all that I was just a rookie. The day ended without our locating Michael.

Day two began much same as every other morning with O.H.—free newspaper, doughnuts, and coffee. But we ended the news and coffee session early and began the hunt for Michael. O.H. had received a tip that would lead us to Michael's mother's house. He drove into a not-so-upscale neighborhood and stopped right in front of a rather rundown house.

"You take the back," O.H. gruffly instructed me.

I trotted around to the rear of the house, around piles of garbage and the rusting hulk of what had formerly been an automobile. It was impossible to get very close to the rear of the house because of all the junk stacked up in the weeds.

Almost immediately I began to hear noises coming from inside the house. It sounded a bit like scuffling, only the noises were moving upward, as if someone was climbing an interior wall. I ran back around the piles of weed-covered junk and found O.H. at the front door.

"O.H., it sounds like someone is trying to climb up into an attic or something," I said.

O.H. gave me a look of contempt and then looked back at a tiny boy standing in the now-open front doorway. I had not even noticed him.

"Michael's not here," the boy said to O.H.

With the same look of contempt he had displayed toward me, O.H. pushed the boy aside and entered a few steps inside the house. Weren't we supposed to have a warrant or something? I thought. But I didn't dare ask the question aloud.

"Come out, Michael!" O.H. shouted toward the ceiling. "We know you're in here!"

I've never forgotten what happened next. Michael, who was indeed trying to hide in the attic, made a mistake in his footing and came crashing through the sheetrock ceiling to land on top of the kitchen stove in a dust-covered heap. *Now, that's how this is supposed to work*, I thought. I guessed that O.H. must have some kind of magical power or authority to make such a thing happen. After I stopped laughing, I handcuffed Michael, and off to juvenile division we went. With O.H.'s help, I had my first felony duck.

Interestingly enough, I met up with O.H. again in 2002, and we got along just fine. This time he needed my help. O.H. no longer had any control over me. I had become the salty old veteran, and I had forgiven him for all the cussing and mistreatment. My desire to get even with O.H. and give him a piece of my mind had lessened, and eventually it left me entirely. Is there a spiritual lesson in here somewhere? Of course there is.

As Christians we are no longer under the control of our sinful flesh. When we came to Christ by faith, our old nature was crucified with Christ. The good news here is that we have been set free from our enslavement to our past. If we sin now, as Christians, it is because we allow it to happen. The Devil can't make us do anything. Jesus has provided us with the victory, and we just need to realize it and live it.

Now, I'm not saying that O.H. was the Devil, but as my training officer, he had control over me, and I didn't like it. I had to get out from under that situation somehow. Rather than give in and become like O.H. or quit the department, I endured and learned what I could from him. I won a small victory there and became a stronger believer and a better officer.

The apostle Paul wrote: "For while we were in the flesh, the sinful passions, which were aroused by the Law, were at work in the members of our body to bear fruit for death. But now we have been released from the Law, having died to that by which we were bound, so that we serve in newness of the Spirit and not in oldness of the letter" (Romans 7:5–6 NASB).

The newness of the Spirit comes when we commit our lives to Christ. It is this newness of the Spirit that enabled me to forgive someone who offended me daily. How do we continue to find that newness each day?

Paul provided us with that answer in Romans 12:1–2 (NASB): "Therefore I urge you, brethren, by the mercies of God, to present your bodies a living and holy sacrifice, acceptable to God, which is your spiritual service of worship. And do not be conformed to this world, but be transformed by the renewing of your mind, so that you may prove what the will of God is, that which is good and acceptable and perfect."

What are the keys to doing this? We begin by presenting ourselves—our bodies and minds—to God, each and every day. I had to yield to God my desire to get even with O.H. for his harsh treatment. I admit that it was difficult to do, but because I had surrendered my life to the lordship of Jesus, I eventually won the struggle.

In your life, Jesus is either Lord *of* all or He isn't Lord *at* all. When we refuse to release our hold on any area of our lives, we are maintaining control and refusing to present ourselves to Jesus' lordship. Today, when you rise from bed and begin your day, yield to God. You might pray something like this: "God, today I pray that You will direct me in all that I do. I present myself to You. Be my Lord and Savior today. Use me as You see fit, and bring Yourself glory. Be with me, Lord, on patrol today."

Rookies

Things change quickly. It seemed that one day I was a rookie, and the next day I was a veteran officer. It was common practice that "floating" rookie officers were assigned to relatively new officers like me. Because rookies were not allowed to patrol alone, the least senior officers were given the responsibility of partnering up for the day. Veteran officers rarely had that responsibility.

The first time I was partnered with a less senior officer than myself, I was a bit nervous. How was I supposed to act with a rookie in my patrol car? I had never been the senior officer before. Should I act serious and not talk to the rookie much during the shift, as some of my senior officers had done to me? Should I talk a lot, like an old friend, and offer as much wisdom as I could? I decided to try to just be myself.

Early in my second year on the job, one rookie asked me whether or not I was the snitch that he had been warned about. I was dumbfounded that a rookie, fresh from the academy, had been warned about me, a senior officer. It was, however, a good opportunity to explain my actions and to talk about integrity and honesty. I would repeat that talk a number of times over the years.

Some rookies who patrolled with me were very good. Some were better than I was at that point in my career. Others were less than prepared for the job. One rookie, for example, who made a mistake on a vehicle tow-away slip, used liquid paper to cover the mistake, forgetting the two carbon copies beneath the first page.

There was a period of time in 1984 in which I was regularly assigned to patrol with a young female rookie I'll call Ski. Although Ski was a pleasant person to talk to, she wasn't very good at the job of being a police officer. In fact, she seemed to have her mind and attention focused somewhere else most of the time. Ski was not very receptive to constructive criticism. I saw a bit of myself in Ski, and wanted to help her become a competent officer. I initially tried dropping subtle hints about her mistakes. When that didn't seem to work, I openly discussed some of her more glaring shortcomings with her. She had to remain focused on the dangerous job at hand.

One fall night, Ski and I were riding shift three out of the Ponderosa station. I was driving, and Ski was riding shotgun. Things were going along quietly, when a small, black car ran a red light in front of us. I made a U-turn and initiated a traffic stop. I approached on the driver's side of the car, as I always did when I had a patrol partner. Since it was a night shift, I had one hand on the grip of my pistol. With the other hand, I blasted a quick beam of light into the eyes of the driver of the car. That quick flash of light temporarily took away the driver's night vision and gave me a slight advantage in the event the violator was a bad guy intending to do me harm.

Ski approached on the passenger side of the violator's car. As I reached the driver's door, I was struck by the impression that the male driver appeared much too large for the little car he was driving. I asked for his driver's license and his insurance papers, and the man began rummaging through the glove compartment of the car. Ski stood outside the passenger window, shining her flashlight inside and looking around, always watching the hands of the violator, just as she had been trained.

After a few brief seconds, the violator suddenly sat straight up in the seat of his car, looked at me, and, as if he had just remembered something important, said, "Oh, I got a piece."

"Huh, you got a what?" was my response.

"A piece," he repeated a bit more loudly.

He must have watched a lot of gangster movies to come up with the word *piece*, but I knew instantly what he meant. I quickly removed the man from his car and handcuffed him. I walked him back to our patrol car, searched him for weapons or other contraband, and placed him into the backseat of our car.

I returned to the violator's car and noticed Ski looking at me with a bewildered, "what-just-happened?" look on her face. I leaned into the man's car, and there, in plain view in the open glove compartment, was a fully loaded handgun. Collecting the firearm and making it safe, I stepped away from the car and held the gun up in front of Ski's face. I asked whether or not she had seen it during the violator's rummaging through the glove compartment.

Ski stuttered and stammered and apologized for missing the gun, a mistake that could have cost us our lives.

I briefly puzzled over how I should handle this. I had made mistakes on patrol myself; I wasn't perfect. But I knew that I could not simply pretend that Ski had not made a serious mistake. If she was receptive, this could be a learning experience that could prove helpful in her growth as a police officer. If not, then she could live to repeat the mistake or lose her life because of it. I hoped for my sake and hers that she would listen and learn.

Eventually I found out the answer to my question about whether or not Ski would learn to focus on the job. She continued to work patrol after I had transferred to another station. Years passed before I heard anything about her. It seemed that she had continued to ignore warnings from other officers, but that all changed for her one night.

Somehow, Ski missed the radio broadcast about an aggravated robbery in her patrol area. The description of the suspects and their getaway vehicle had been broadcast over the radio to all officers in the district in what was referred to as a "general broadcast," or GB. All was quiet, until a call from a citizen came in about an officer who was down and likely dead behind a strip center. The dispatcher dropped an "assist the officer" call, and all available units responded.

The first unit to arrive found Ski facedown in a pool of blood. No one even knew that Ski was missing or that she had stopped the robbery suspect's car. She had broken the most basic safety rules in the book, and now she was seriously injured. Ski had not notified the dispatcher or other units where she was or what she was about to do. She apparently didn't realize who she was stopping. Ski had missed all the warnings, and although she had been taught and trained by some of the best, she had failed to follow basic safety rules.

Months later, Ski managed to recover enough from her injuries to be released from the hospital. Shortly after that, she resigned from the department and moved away. She became a schoolteacher somewhere up north, or so I've heard.

What do we take away from this? What spiritual lesson would God have us learn out on patrol? It seems too simple to say that the Scriptures are the rule book for our lives, which is why they contain the laws, ordinances, and statutes of God; but it is true. Everything we need to survive spiritually is found in the Bible. We have the lessons and teachings from those who have gone before us to help us stay away from danger. There are books, pastors, Sunday school teachers, retreats, seminars, and many more resources that provide the training and warnings we need. Why, then, do we sometimes find ourselves in a life-and-death struggle for which we are ill prepared to survive?

David was king of Israel when he found himself in a similar situation with a woman named Bathsheba. David was at home, instead of being out on the field of battle with his men (2 Samuel 11). He went up on the rooftop, and there she was. It was a moment of truth for David, and he failed miserably.

We all find ourselves at physical or spiritual moments of truth in our lives, perhaps many times. Our focus and preparation play a part in the outcome. It is important to always remember that we have an adversary who seeks to destroy us. A warning is found in 1 Peter 5:8 (NASB): "Be of sober spirit, be on the alert. Your adversary, the devil, prowls around like a roaring lion, seeking someone to devour."

I believe that law enforcement officers are often used by God as His warning device to others. Officers often lecture people, and just as often, I've heard those people complain about being lectured. In my view, such lectures are warnings that should be listened to.

Are you ignoring warning signs? Has someone recently sounded the alarm in your life? If so, please listen and do not allow your pride to keep you from benefitting. Understand that the alarm is sounded out of love and concern for you.

9

PONDEROSA AND THE CHASE

Riding the night shift is significantly different from day and evening shifts—in more ways than just the fact that it is dark outside. There are things that happen after sunset, and people who seem only to venture out after dark, that make it a somewhat surreal experience.

    Early in my career, my wife and I purchased a home northwest of Houston, making the drive to Westside Station a bit too far. As a result, I transferred to a patrol station that was nicknamed "the Ponderosa." I'm not sure how or why it earned that name, but the Ponderosa was considered a retirement station because nothing ever seemed to happen there. At Westside, I had worked with many officers who were motivated, proactive, and some of the youngest and best the department had to offer.

    In the early 1980s, I found that the Ponderosa differed dramatically from Westside. That difference was not just in the ages of the officers but in their attitudes. My first night at the Ponderosa warned me of things to come. I was standing in line outside the radio room after roll call. All stations had a radio room, a bit of hallowed ground, where the officer who worked it was in charge of handing out the patrol car keys and radios. To anger or upset him in any way meant that you ended up driving a clunker that night. As I reached the doorway and stood waiting for a radio and car keys, the officer in charge looked at me and then down at a copy of the shift roster. Then, looking back at me, he said, "Just because you come from Westside, don't think you need to be out there running calls and catching criminals. We don't want to hear you on the air. We do things differently around here." That seemed a bit harsh to me.

What I didn't know until after I had transferred away from the Ponderosa a year and a half later was that I had been branded a "snitch" because of my honesty in the brutality complaint during my field training time three years earlier. Word had been passed to the Ponderosa that I was transferring in, and they were expected to make life miserable for me. I must say, they did a good job of it too. In fact, the only people I could consider friends were other outcasts. The night shift commander—I'll call him Lieutenant Five—held a rather good-ol'-boys view of life. He felt that female officers should work the desk, where he could keep an eye on them, and they could make coffee and look pretty. Five was not only a sexist, but he was also an open racist, who loudly stated one night that one of the African-American officers should be taken fishing, dragged behind the boat as alligator bait. Complaints were filed against Five for this idiotic statement, and an Internal Affairs Division investigation resulted in a short suspension with loss of pay.

Five had also heard that a snitch was transferring in, and he felt it was his responsibility to rid the department of another troublemaker. I could spend several pages describing the things that Five did in response to my transfer and in defense of his previously unchallenged authority. One example was when Five formed "The Committee," made up of several senior officers, to put pressure on any officer he deemed as trouble.

One night, Five sent "The Committee" around the station with a letter that he had authored himself, a letter of support that was meant to counter the complaint against him for racism. All who refused to sign their names in support would be harassed unmercifully until they did sign. Signing the support letter for Five could have meant a positive change for me because in their eyes, I would have been on their side—not the troublemaking snitch they had heard about. This was a chance for me to become one of the guys, to finally fit in. After all, he hadn't done much to me that was negative—yet. That fight wasn't even mine, was it?

I do not want to present myself as some super Christian here, because in reality, my initial intention was to remain neutral, to be left alone to work. I had not forgotten the lessons learned after the brutality complaint years earlier. But neutrality and acceptance evaded me.

In matters of injustice, I do not find neutrality condoned in Scripture. No one truly remains neutral when it comes to injustice. To keep silent is to condone it. The dividing lines for those who are in Christ have been done away with. Galatians 3:28 (NASB) says, "There is neither Jew nor Greek, there is neither slave nor free man, there is neither male nor female; for you are all one in Christ Jesus." Racism is unacceptable, and try as we may, no Christian remains neutral on the issue. However, we often try to reestablish the dividing lines through our denominations, politics, or ethnicity. We look to fit in, and we often alienate those we should be reaching or protecting.

Jesus' words in Matthew 12:30 (NASB) indicate that there are only two sides on which to be found: His side or the other side. Look at His words: "He who is not with Me is against Me; and he who does not gather with Me scatters." What is not found here is a middle ground of neutrality.

For those in law enforcement, the pressure to fit in can be tremendous. When your life is literally dependent upon your coworkers daily, you tend to want to be liked, respected, and well-spoken of.

The Chase

Shortly after "The Committee" circulated the support letter, which I refused to sign, I found myself feeling alone and rather unblessed because of snide remarks and attitudes of some of my coworkers. No one wanted to ride with the religious guy, whom they had been led to believe would try to snitch on them at every opportunity. My desire was to do the right thing, to take the course of action I believed was pleasing to the Lord in each situation, and to just do my job. The apostle Paul wrote to Timothy these words, "Indeed, all who desire to live godly in Christ Jesus will be persecuted" (2 Timothy 3:12 NASB). I felt that I was experiencing a taste of that verse each night I reported for duty.

Five sent me to a Traffic Enforcement Specialist school that included radar certification and commercial truck inspection, perhaps thinking that he was punishing me. One night, while I was looking for traffic violators, a patrol unit notified the dispatcher that they were in pursuit of a pickup truck. The unit in pursuit was made up of two officers. One was the regular beat officer, and the other was a desk officer who rode the street one night a week to write traffic citations in order to earn overtime pay for attending traffic court.

The chase was nearby, so I headed that way and joined in the pursuit. I was not driving a radar car that night; as was the custom, they had given the snitch the worst clunker of a car they had. I puttered along, trying to catch up to the chase. The primary unit was in pursuit of a white pickup truck, and the guy driving it was trying to get away at all costs.

We circled a local hospital and headed back to the interstate, where the truck turned west on the eastbound I-10 feeder road. He accelerated and entered the freeway via the exit ramp. Now we were going the wrong way on Interstate 10 in the middle of the night. The crook moved to the far inside lane, going the wrong way, which was already insane, but then he turned his headlights off. There did not seem to be any way this pursuit was going to end well.

Interstate 10 is one of the most heavily traveled Interstates connecting the east and west coasts of the United States. Exceeding ninety miles per hour and traveling in the wrong direction, traffic flashed by our windows at incredible speeds.

My mind was racing with questions like, "Are you crazy?" and "What are you doing?" Even knowing that the chase was a bad idea, I continued on. I couldn't let those officers catch the crook and have them label me a coward on top of the snitch label. Somehow I had forgotten that Bible verse about pride going before a fall—or perhaps a fatal car crash.

We continued the chase. Not getting hit head-on was a miracle. The white pickup exited the freeway several miles down I-10, made a quick U-turn, and headed back east on the service road. Another patrol car cut in front of the truck in an attempt to force him into a construction area where we could surround him. The truck accelerated, trying to reenter the freeway, but it collided with construction equipment. A huge cloud of dust exploded, temporarily concealing the truck from view. The truck exited the dust cloud, upside-down, sliding on its roof.

Each of us in turn began to brake hard as we cleared the cloud of dust. Over the screaming sirens and radio traffic, I heard the primary unit calling for an ambulance and advising the dispatcher and other units that the suspect had "cracked up." The assumption was that the crook would be injured and in need of emergency first aid. No sooner had those words gone out over the air than I saw, to my disbelief, the crook crawl out of his upside-down truck and begin to run across the freeway. He jumped the center divider wall and ran across four lanes of oncoming westbound traffic.

We left our cars running, lights flashing and some with sirens still blaring, as we began the foot pursuit. The sound of the sirens became faint as we distanced ourselves from the crash site. Over the dividing wall we went, somehow managing to avoid being struck by a westbound vehicle. We ran, gasping for air, our flashlights throwing erratic beams of light, as we caught fleeting glimpses of our quarry ahead of us. Down a grassy hill we ran and into some type of storage area for heavy construction equipment. Our next obstacle was a barbed-wire fence, but there was no time to stop. The air was filled with sounds of heavy breathing and officers' equipment rattling with each heavy step. The primary unit was right ahead of me. The first officer, who was a bit out of shape, became entangled in the barbed wire and fell to the ground. The rest of us continued the chase, leaving the officer to untangle himself.

Now, the only officer ahead of me in the foot chase was the desk officer, who promptly fell to the ground as he tripped over something in the grass. On pure adrenaline, I ran after my quarry like a cheetah chasing a gazelle on one of those African wildlife documentaries. In my mind, I felt as if I needed to prove myself to these officers. I foolishly threw caution to the wind.

We cut through a very dark stand of trees. Light from the interstate no longer reached us. I was out of breath, gasping, trying to fill my lungs, which strained against the restriction of the body armor I wore. Emerging from the trees, I spotted the driver of the truck just yards ahead of me and cutting to my right. As I closed in on him, the police helicopter that had been following the chase the entire time descended out of nowhere to a hover just feet above the ground, cutting off the man's escape route. That was something I had never seen before. The violator's momentary pause allowed me to close the distance. I crashed into him, and we both went to the ground hard.

That was the first time I had crashed into anyone since I'd played little league football. But on this occasion, I was not wearing protective padding, and the man I had crashed into wasn't a ball carrier but someone who desperately wanted to escape capture. Did I mention that he was much larger than me? Most people were.

On the ground, we began to grapple, each of us attempting to take control of the other. Somehow, over the noise of the helicopter, which was now ascending and disappearing back into the dark night sky, I could hear the helicopter observer advising the dispatcher and other responding units over the radio that the suspect was in custody. I disagreed.

Our struggle continued. The desk officer arrived and managed to apply handcuffs to one of the crook's wrists. With one violent movement, the loose end of the handcuffs caught the desk officer on the forehead, which opened up a deep gash. It quickly became apparent that the crook was not only larger than me, but stronger as well. I grabbed him around the neck, locking on to him, and swung my flashlight with all my might, attempting to knock him off-balance as he tried to stand up. The thought that I needed to begin lifting weights crossed my mind.

The crook shouted at me rather calmly, "Stop hitting me," and grabbed my flashlight.

My tactics were not working, as we now struggled for control of the flashlight. He attempted to take it away from me, and I summoned up all the strength I could to keep it in my possession. If he got my light, he could kill me with it. He had already drawn blood on the desk officer, who was now out of the fight.

About this time, I saw beams from a dozen flashlights moving across the area. Other officers were looking for us, but the tall grass hid us from their sight. With all that I had, I managed to twist my flashlight from the crook's hands, keeping my left arm around his neck. I held the light as high as I could with my right hand and clicked it on and off in the direction of the searching officers.

I heard someone shout, "There they are!" The crowd of officers came charging in, piling on top of us. I released my grip on the crook and pushed myself away from the pile.

I can't really say what I expected to happen next. Maybe a congratulatory word or two were in order, or perhaps a pat on the back. With the crook now fully in custody, we all began the walk back to the edge of the freeway, criminal in tow. An ambulance sat on the shoulder, loading up the primary unit's officer, who had fallen on the fence and sustained a back injury.

Five had arrived at the scene. With excitement, he asked what had happened, said "way to go," and so on. Five was congratulating the desk officer, when, much to my surprise, he said, "It was Caronna that caught him." Five looked at me, and the smile faded from his face. His smile was replaced by a look of disgust, or perhaps disappointment. It was as if I had ruined the night for him. Without a word, he turned away and told everyone to head back to the other side of the freeway to where the crook's truck still sat upside down.

Everyone loaded up quickly into a few patrol cars and drove away, leaving me standing alone. No one offered me a ride. I had to run back across the westbound side of the freeway to reach the other side. At that point, anger began to rise within me. How could they treat me this way? I had performed like a veteran officer. I had caught the bad guy, risked life and limb, and still I was not one of the guys. By the time I reached my patrol car, I was fuming. I would need to look within for the lesson.

Spiritually, we are in a battle every day, whether we feel like it or not. I had just experienced a physical battle, not unlike the spiritual one we wage against spiritual forces. Ephesians 6:12 (NASB) tells us, "For our struggle is not against flesh and blood, but against the rulers, against the powers, against the world forces of this darkness, against the spiritual forces of wickedness in the heavenly places."

During the physical struggle that night, I'd had my light, and I had attempted to use it effectively to alert others and to stop the criminal. He had tried to take my light away from me, something I could not allow.

The spiritual parallel is that there is a dark and dying world all around us. People are searching for truth, for something or someone to believe in, but they are in darkness.

We Christians have the Light. The truth of God's Word is the Light. When we live inconsistent lives, our light dims, and people cannot see the truth of the gospel. In fact, they turn away at our hypocrisy, and our spiritual enemy gets the victory. In reality, Five was not my enemy, although he acted as if he was. If I allowed anger to take control, I would stop trying, and my light would go out. I had to remember that my calling was not to find a way to fit in and be one of the guys, but rather to continue to please God.

Are you shining the light, or are you consumed by a desire to fit in?

Where's the Fire?

Not everything I experienced on patrol was negative. I have many good memories, and I made some good friendships that have lasted for years.

One of the most eye-opening things I found when I entered police work was the strange behavior of people and the excuses they made when they were caught misbehaving. Nowhere was this more obvious or frequent than when conducting traffic stops. I get a little bothered when I hear someone use the phrase "routine traffic stop." While I understand their intent, it is often anything but routine.

When I was made a radar unit, I did my best to fulfill those duties, even though I preferred to be out running calls for service and looking for bad guys. Often, a traffic violator would ask the question, "Why aren't you out looking for real criminals instead of hassling me?" My usual response to that question was, "If you would drive in a safe manner, I could do just that, but because you chose to run that red light (or speed), I had to leave my search for real criminals to make the streets safe from you"—or something to that effect.

Interestingly enough, real criminals drive cars too, and they often violate traffic laws like any other motorist. Does the name Timothy McVeigh, the Oklahoma City terrorist bomber, ring a bell? He was stopped for driving without a license plate and was arrested for a weapons violation within ninety minutes of the bombing.

When it comes to the more common traffic violations, such as speeding, the excuses can be rather humorous. A frequent explanation from female motorists who exceeded the posted speed limit was, "Officer, I had to go to the bathroom, and there are no clean bathrooms around here."

I stopped one young motorist for speeding, and he repeatedly put his hand up to his nose and then looked at his hand. When I asked him the reason why he was traveling so fast, he responded, "Well, you see, officer, I sometimes get nosebleeds, and I felt one coming on. Since I don't have any tissue in the car, I was speeding home for one so I wouldn't get blood in my car."

Yeah, right. Sure you were.

Another lady told me she ran a red light because, as she put it, "I was in a dilemma zone."

"A what zone?" I asked.

"You know, a dilemma zone, where the light is changing from green to yellow, and you don't know whether to speed up, hoping to make it before it turns red, or to slam on the brakes and hope no one rear-ends you."

One night I stopped a pickup truck that I had clocked speeding. As I approached the truck, I noticed that both the inspection sticker and registration were expired. The driver, a middle-aged woman, appeared distraught. I began with my usual questions, and when I asked her the reason why she was speeding, the woman said through tears, "Because my dog had a heart attack." That was something new. I didn't see a dog in her truck, so I asked where the dog was.

"I dropped him off at the emergency clinic," she replied.

"Okay, the emergency is over now. So, why are you driving so fast?" I asked a second time.

"Because I'm driving with my left foot," was her answer. Okay, this was getting interesting. I looked into the truck and noticed that her right foot had only a sock and was way over to the right of the pedals. Her left foot, with a shoe on it, was pressing on the brake pedal. The next logical question would be why she was driving with her left foot.

"Because I fell off a seven-foot-tall brick wall. Officer, you just don't know what I have been going through." I left it at that.

Some traffic stops were humorous, and some were not. There was the time I approached on the passenger side of a vehicle, and the passenger, who was looking for me on the driver's side of the car, dropped a little baggie of cocaine out the window, thinking I wouldn't see it. It landed on my boots.

God always protected me during these stops, but it was never as obvious as it was one night on Houston's near north side. I was riding evening shift out of the Central Patrol Division, when I pulled into a North Main Street parking lot to catch up on some paperwork. It was dark out, and I was tired. I almost didn't see the body in time.

I slammed on the brakes just before rolling over an intoxicated man who was lying on the dark pavement. I advised the dispatcher of my location and exited my patrol car. The man was very intoxicated, so I decided that he needed a night in the jailhouse to sober up. He would be much safer there than he was on the pavement. I helped the man lean forward against the side of the patrol car to help balance him while I searched him for weapons.

I was about halfway through the search, when I saw some movement out of the corner of my eye. I looked up in time to see the figure of a man running around the corner of a building several yards away. I concluded the search and placed the intoxicated man into the back of my patrol car. When I turned away from my car, I saw a well-dressed man wearing an apron. He was several feet away and approached me with a concerned look on his face.

He spoke with a trembling voice. "Officer, I thought that man was going to shoot you."

"What man?" I asked, thinking of the highly intoxicated man now sitting in the backseat of the patrol car.

"That man that just ran around the corner," he replied. "We removed him from our restaurant." He pointed to the nearby establishment. "I escorted him out and watched him. He walked up to you and pulled a handgun out of his pocket. He pointed it at the back of your head while you were searching that other man. He just paused there for a second, and then he lowered his arm and ran away."

I was stunned. I searched for the gunman but was unable to locate him.

When we place our faith in Christ Jesus, an intimate relationship with God is established. We are adopted into His family, and even when we are not thinking about God, when we are working and totally focused on our jobs, families, or hobbies, God is with us. This doesn't mean that no harm will ever come to us. Many faithful Christians have been martyred for their faith. I do believe that it means that nothing can enter our lives that God will not ultimately use for our good. While I have experienced times of doubt or uncertainty, I base that previous statement upon this promise from God's Word: "And we know that God causes all things to work together for good to those who love God, to those who are called according to His purpose" (Romans 8:28 NASB).

Notice that the Scripture doesn't say that all things *are* good but that God causes all things to *work together* for good. God wasn't finished with me that night. He still isn't. When will my days be finished, my number up? I don't know, and neither do you. What I learned on patrol that night is to live for God now. Every moment, live and love. Love God. Love your family, your children, and your friends. Tell them that you love them. Make the most of what time God has given you, and don't live with regret over unfinished business, forgiveness withheld, or unspoken words.

How will you respond when something negative comes your way?

Caught Red-Handed

Over the years, I have arrested a lot of people. Some arrests were for serious crimes, such as sexual assault, aggravated robbery, or even murder. Some arrests were for less serious crimes, including traffic offenses.

In the Old Testament book of Numbers, Moses gave instructions to God's people, telling them what God expected and required of them. In a discussion with the sons of Gad and Reuben, Moses spoke a warning that each of us would do well to remember: "But if you will not do so, behold, you have sinned against the LORD, and be sure your sin will find you out" (Numbers 32:23 NASB).

Those of us who claim to be believers in Jesus Christ are expected to follow Him, to obey Him, to love Him. When we disobey, Christ calls us to repent of our sin. If we refuse, we can be certain that we will face God's chastisement, sometimes to our embarrassment in front of others. The following two stories are what I consider to be examples of one's sin being found out.

Night shift at the Ponderosa could be very slow and boring. However, the area had been experiencing a series of sexual assaults, and on one particularly slow night, I began looking for the culprit. I had a rookie riding with me that night, and although I didn't know him well, he seemed to be a good one. We began cruising remote parking lots and out-of-the-way areas, looking for anything out-of-the-ordinary.

While cruising one deserted stretch of roadway, I noticed a single automobile backed into a spot at the far end of a parking lot of a closed business. Behind the parking lot was a large, wooded area. I turned off the patrol car headlights and told the rookie what I was about to do. We cruised into the parking lot slowly, quietly, all lights turned off. We approached the car like some kind of predator attempting to get within range before leaping. The car appeared to be empty.

I shifted into neutral and coasted closer, closer. I then cut the engine and gently pressed the emergency brake in order to keep the brake lights from activating as we came to a stop. We exited our patrol car, leaving the doors open, and approached the abandoned car on foot. I wanted desperately to catch the serial rapist. I also still wanted to gain the respect of those who saw me only as a snitch, or perhaps I just wanted to prove them wrong.

The car was empty, but the hood was still warm. It was too far from the building to have anything to do with legitimate business there. I signaled the rookie to move toward the dark woods—no talking now—just listening and moving slowly forward. We listened for voices, movement, anything that would give away the location of the person who had parked the car.

Sensing that someone was in front of us, and hearing muffled sounds, we both switched on our flashlights—20,000-candlepower times two—to find a blanket occupied by a man and a woman. Have you ever heard the phrase "like a deer caught in the headlights"? Well, here were a dear and a baboon, right there in living color.

No, it wasn't a rape in progress. They were there consensually. We escorted them back to their car to obtain some identification and to find out why they were there. I mean, I knew *why* they were there, but I wanted to know why they were *there*.

When we reached the car, I noticed something I hadn't seen when we'd first approached it. Taped to the rear window, from inside the car, was an advertisement—some kind of flyer. Looking more closely, I noticed that it advertised revival services at a familiar church. With no concern for political correctness, I began to ask the man about the flyer.

"Is this your car?" I asked.

"Yes, sir," he responded.

"Are you a member of the church in that flyer on your window?"

"Yes, sir," he answered rather sheepishly.

"Is this woman with you your wife?"

"Uh, no, sir," he responded, now looking directly at the ground in front of him.

I wanted to stop questioning him. I mean, who was I to ask these kinds of questions? I was a cop, and I must ask cop-type questions, right?

Before, during, and after my police career, I was, am, and will be a Christian. As such, I must allow myself to be used by God as He sees fit. That night, God used me to bring conviction to the life of one of His own—conviction for sin; conviction for taking a woman who was a visitor at his church and who was not his wife and becoming sexually involved with her; conviction for ruining his witness and bringing shame to the name of Christ.

You see, that man had been faced with temptation, as we all are. He wasn't in sin because of temptation but because he chose to give in to the temptation by entering into a sinful relationship with a woman to whom he was not married. He thought he was safe there in his hiding place, but his sin found him out. He was exposed—pardon the pun. If he believed that his act was not sinful, then why did he feel the need to locate a remote wooded spot, park his car as far from the roadway as he could, and hide in the darkness with the object of his lust? He had placed both himself and the woman with him in danger just by being there. You can guess how the rest of the interview with the man went that night.

I struggled with whether or not I had done the right thing in questioning the man. The rookie, however, thought it was funny. He had no idea that God was chastening one of His children and was using me to do it. I felt humbled, almost embarrassed, knowing that it could just as easily have been me there getting caught, had I not taken God out on patrol with me.

The second story occurred years later. I had finally transferred away from the Ponderosa. My last night there was an eye-opener. The radio room officer confessed to me that the reason I had been so harassed by Five and the other officers was due to the snitch incident. He confessed to me that he had watched me for a year and a half and had never seen me do anything that could justify my receiving such poor treatment. It was his way of apologizing, I guess. Anyway, I was riding night shift in One District with a relatively new female partner. We rode unit 1A25N.

"1 Adam 25?"

"1 Adam 25. Go ahead, ma'am."

"1A25, check the loud noise disturbance at the Diamond News Stand, 12832 Richmond Ave. Code two."

I had previously learned that the Diamond News Stand didn't sell newspapers in One District. It sold pornography. It sold every kind of magazine, video, and other paraphernalia—imaginable and unimaginable—that most folks would rather not know about. This area of town was peppered with these types of businesses. Most of these businesses contained a retail sales area—and a less obvious arcade area behind locked doors, usually down dark, narrow hallways. My partner and I had been inside several of these places on our patrols of the district.

We arrived at the newsstand and immediately felt that something seemed wrong. A loud-noise call at this type of establishment was odd in itself. We entered the parking lot, already thinking that something out-of-the-ordinary was going on there. The second thing that seemed out-of-place was the window in the front door. A window that allowed the store clerk to see outside into the parking lot wasn't all that odd, but this window also allowed us to see inside the store, which was unusual. These clerks wanted to know who was coming in the door, so they could warn the patrons of the arcade if the police arrived.

Something I had difficulty learning when I entered police work was "command bearing." Essentially, "command bearing" is body language that says, when you arrive on a scene, that you are the man—I mean, *The Man*. You are in charge and must act like it in order to maintain or obtain order and control of a situation. To avoid danger and to protect yourself and others, you must take control quickly. You cannot be shy or timid. You must be courteously forceful and stern, without being abusive and rude.

Anyway, let's get back to the story. We entered the common store area, and as my partner engaged (distracted) the clerk, I headed straight for the doorway leading into the arcade area. The only problem was that the door was locked and could only be opened remotely by the clerk. I grasped the door handle firmly, turned back to the clerk, and, with all the command bearing I could muster, shouted, "Open the door!" The door buzzed, and we both went through it, splitting up to cover two hallways.

Let me quickly describe this place to you. It was a dark, narrow hallway with many closed doors on each side, like a hotel. As we began forcing open doors to little rooms, the hallway lights came on, and men began exiting the little rooms in various stages of undress, like cockroaches scattering when lights come on in a kitchen. Each little room contained a token-operated video machine. I proceeded quickly from room to room, but it seemed that each room had already emptied of its occupants.

Suddenly I heard my partner's excited voice shouting, "Mark, I got one in here!" I ran around the corner of the hallway and immediately saw her leaning hard against a door, trying to open it, as someone on the inside tried even harder to close it, pinning her between the door and the frame. I buried my shoulder into the door, and together we began to force the door open. There was an audible crack as we forced the door open, pinning someone behind it.

A voice from behind the door said, "Okay, okay, I'll stop. Just let me get dressed, please."

We looked at each other, wondering what exactly we had pinned behind the door. We eased up the pressure, and a very large man stepped out from behind the door. Now, I won't go into a lot of details on what we saw here, but let me just say that what goes on in those places would probably make the inhabitants of Sodom blush.

We arrested the big man for public lewdness. He immediately began trying to explain his behavior, whining and crying about being embarrassed and claiming that he had never done anything like this before. Before we towed away his gold Mercedes Benz from the parking lot, a property inventory of the vehicle revealed numerous arcade tokens in the trunk—proof that this was not his first time at Diamond News. He'd never done that before? Yeah, right.

The man turned out to be a successful local attorney with a wife and children at home. He had hosted a dinner party at his home earlier in the evening and had volunteered to be the designated driver. On his way back home, where his wife and children waited, he decided to indulge in his secret sin. No one in his family knew about this secret. However, now his sins had found him out, and it wasn't going to be a secret anymore. Everyone else in his life would know—his law partners, his wife, his parents, and his children. He asked me how he should handle the predicament he was now in, which I found interesting.

I took this experience as a reminder—not that God was coldly watching people and waiting for them to mess up so He could embarrass them, but that my heavenly Father loved me enough to remind me that, although sin may seem like fun, it comes at great cost. Any one of us—however strong and above this kind of behavior we may think ourselves to be—are subject to failure.

"Therefore let him who thinks he stands take heed that he does not fall" (1 Corinthians 10:12 NASB). The best way to keep from falling into sin is to abide in Christ and walk in the Spirit, so as not to fulfill the lusts of the flesh (Galatians 5:16). Additionally, we must consciously avoid placing ourselves into situations where we are likely to fall. If you already know that you have a weakness, then avoid those people, places, or situations where you are going to face what tempts you.

You do not get to choose what tempts you, but you do have a choice in how you respond when you are tempted. Allow God to be in control of your life every moment of every day, and find your strength in Him. Understand where you are weak, and move to where you are strong.

12

DEALING WITH DEATH

In this life, all that we can be certain of are death and taxes. Have you ever heard that before? Have you ever said it? I can add that I am certain of my salvation and a future in a place called heaven with a heavenly Father who loves me. I am also certain that I love my family and that they love me. There will be no death or taxes in heaven. Death, however, is one appointment we all must keep, and none of us will be late for it. "And just as it is appointed for man to die once, and after that comes judgment" (Hebrews 9:27 ESV).

It is an unfortunate reality that police officers, as well as paramedics and firefighters, encounter death often, and most often it is death resulting from unnatural causes. Most first-responders develop coping mechanisms that allow them to continue their work in the face of overwhelming tragedy and death without being overcome with emotion. These coping mechanisms can at times make first-responders seem insensitive or uncaring.

In police work, there are a few phrases that are commonly used to describe how a person appears to have died. Since we respond frequently to calls related to death, we often use these descriptive phrases and slang terms. There is the *natural*, which refers to a death that is apparently due to natural causes. *Floater* describes a body found in water. A body found in varying stages of decomposition is often referred to as a *stinker*. As I said, it can seem insensitive, but it brings to mind the story of Lazarus in John 11.

I realize how crass this reads, but let me tell you that I have seen people who have died in every way imaginable, and even years later, I wish that I hadn't. I wish that I could unsee and forget what I have seen. Every first-responder could say the same thing. There is a myth that men and women responding to emergency calls are able to handle it all because it is part of the job; it's what they are trained and paid for. However, just as no soldier comes back from combat unchanged, neither does a first-responder go through a career without being changed to some degree by what he or she has experienced.

To keep things in perspective, we realize that a human body is simply a temporary vessel that carries the real person throughout his or her time on earth. Bodies die and decay, but the spirit lives on.

Over the years, I have run many calls regarding deceased, injured, or missing people. There are some that I will not likely forget very soon, and one of them in particular that I never will completely forget.

I was assigned to a patrol beat bordered by the North 610 Loop, when I received a call regarding a DOA (dead on arrival). The location was a nice older home with a well-kept yard. This could have been the home of any number of people I knew and loved. I entered through the front door and, along with EMS (emergency medical services), began searching the house. Everything appeared to be in order. There were no signs of foul play or forced entry.

Everything seemed normal, until we entered the master bedroom, where we found two twin beds, side-by-side, neatly made. On one bed was an opened white box. Inside the box was a beautiful dress with matching shoes. On top of the dress was a handwritten letter with instructions for a funeral service.

On the second bed was something I will never forget. A tiny, frail woman lay there on her back, perfectly still, with her hands folded across her abdomen. She was fully clothed and would have appeared to be sleeping, except for one thing. Over her head was a clear plastic bag. The bag was closed off around her neck with a series of small wires linked together. They were the same wires that are used to close off a loaf of bread to keep it fresh. The little woman had simply suffocated herself to death. The letter explained her actions to her family members.

Why? Why did she do this to herself? How could someone suffocate himself or herself like that? In her letter, she explained her loneliness since losing her husband years earlier. The first bed had been his. She had felt despair and a lack of purpose; her life no longer had meaning. She had set out the clothing she wanted to wear in her casket, placed a bag over her own head, sealed it off, and lain down to die. I was stunned by just how lonely she must have been to slowly suffocate herself to death. The natural fight-or-flight response would normally cause a person to fight for breath, to live. I did not understand this level of despair. This little lady's loneliness must have been absolute and all-consuming in her life.

What could I learn from a tragic scene like this? What could God teach me, and what can I share with you?

We live in an age of instant gratification. We enter a fast-food drive-through and become impatient as we sit for a few minutes in our air-conditioned car. Somewhere, we have lost the concept of patience and have replaced it with an overinflated value of ourselves and our time. We are too busy; our days are too full. However, I believe that we make time for what is most important to us.

All around us, people are hurting, searching for purpose and for answers to difficult questions. Many of us rarely take any time from our day to reach out to those who are most at-risk. John 3:16 (NASB), likely the most often quoted Bible verse, reads, "For God so loved the world that He gave His only begotten Son, that whoever believes in Him shall not perish, but have eternal life." This is the message of hope.

Perhaps you need to share that message with someone. Or perhaps that message is for you. Perhaps you are reading this and don't even know that God, the Creator of everything, loves you. In fact, He loves you so much that He would rather die than be separated from you. Call on Jesus right now. Surrender your life to Him, and seek His forgiveness for your sins.

Take comfort in these verses: "And I saw the holy city, new Jerusalem, coming down out of heaven from God, made ready as a bride adorned for her husband. And I heard a loud voice from the throne, saying, "Behold, the tabernacle of God is among men, and He will dwell among them, and they shall be His people, and God Himself will be among them, and He will wipe away every tear from their eyes; and there will no longer be any death; there will no longer be any mourning, or crying, or pain; the first things have passed away" (Revelation 21:2–4 NASB).

13

Shine Your Light

For three years, my regular shift was "late side nights," which meant that my shift began at 11:00 p.m. and ended at 7:00 a.m. the next morning. Like most officers in those days, I worked the "655" overtime program. The mayor at that time had promised to put 655 new officers on the streets. To accomplish that, he budgeted a large amount of money for patrol officers to work overtime. This provided no new officers—just the same old, tired ones, who worked longer days until the training academy could eventually train enough new officers. Like many officers, I either worked one of my regular off days each week, or I came in early and worked four additional hours before my regular shift began.

One particular night, I was working a six-hour slot on my regular day off. In the old Fourth Ward neighborhood, a string of robberies had been perpetrated by the same suspect. His MO (method of operation) was to rob elderly people at shotgun point. These robberies eventually escalated in violence to include a shotgun butt-stroke to the head of his elderly victims. Fortunately, he had not killed any of his victims—yet.

This particular crook was actually a juvenile at the time he committed these crimes, meaning that he was younger than seventeen years of age. He was an average-size kid with one distinguishing feature. He had a fat little chipmunk face, which had earned him the nickname Cheeks. I had never seen Cheeks, but other officers on the beat had. In fact, they had unsuccessfully chased Cheeks on foot a number of times. This frustrated all of us who patrolled the area. Cheeks knew many people in the neighborhood, and they always provided him a hideout.

It was around 2200 hours (10:00 p.m.) when I was called by a fellow officer to meet up at a secure location. When I arrived, Duff told me that he had been informed by a CI (citizen informant) that Cheeks was with another male in an alleyway just south of Andrews Street. Duff's plan was to approach from two different streets as quietly as we could, in order to box Cheeks in. Duff would inform the dispatcher.

Duff and I switched our radios to a car-to-car radio channel that would allow us to talk without interfering with the regular patrol radio channel traffic. The drawback to this was that no one on the regular channel could hear us unless they were in very close proximity. If trouble arose, we would have to switch back to the regular radio channel to call for help. This could be difficult to do in a scuffle in the dark.

We cruised slowly in parallel down two streets. Duff was one block south of the alley, and I was one street north of the alley. I had barely reached the point where I was supposed to stop, when I saw someone run out of the alleyway and nearly collide into the side of my car. Although I had never seen him before, this was obviously Cheeks.

I bailed out of my patrol car, and the foot chase began. I had not yet switched over my handheld radio to channel eight, so I was able to broadcast the foot chase to all cars immediately. I felt rather proud of myself as I ran, broadcasting the chase calmly and clearly. I was even gaining on Cheeks, who was half my age. The problem here was that, unbeknownst to me, Duff was shouting out a foot chase too, on the same channel—only he was chasing the wrong guy. What this meant was that no one heard my broadcast, so no one knew that I was in a foot chase. This was about to become a really bad problem for me.

I ran around houses and across streets, gradually closing in on Cheeks. Suddenly he began yelling, "Grandma, grandma, grandma," as he ran toward the front of a small wood-frame house. I was only an arm's length away, when Cheeks climbed onto the porch of the house, still yelling. Things seemed to slow down for a moment as we ran. I recall seeing a young woman on the front porch, grabbing and twisting the doorknob, also yelling for "grandma" to open the door.

My fingertips were just reaching Cheeks, when we collided because of the still-closed front door. Things sped up then, as we crashed into the door, which popped open and spilled us into the house. We tumbled into a narrow hallway, which, for some reason, contained a single-size mattress and box spring. Cheeks grabbed onto the mattress as if his life depended on it. I grabbed onto the back of his britches and attempted to jerk both Cheeks and the mattress up and out the door we had just crashed through.

What happened next can only be described as chaotic. Someone closed the front door, and two women began screaming at me to release Cheeks, all the while smacking me around with all they had. I was doing my best to push them away, hold onto Cheeks, and get back out of the house alive—all at the same time. I managed to key my radio mike and shout for help. I didn't know the exact address of the house I was in, but I knew the hundred-block, street name, and description of the house. I yelled this information over the radio while maintaining my hold on Cheeks.

I noticed blood on the hands of the woman on my left, as I shoved her away again. I did not know at the time that it was my blood. I yelled at the woman on my right to open the front door. She refused and continued her assault on my right side. I heard over my radio that officers were looking for me but were unable to locate me. I knew that I had to get that door open and get out of the house if I was going to survive this ordeal, but for some reason, I could not force myself to release my grip on Cheeks. The old need for approval from my fellow officers was again rearing its ugly head.

My thoughts were racing. *Why not let go and get out of here? You are going to die in here, and for what—this fat-faced crook? No, you can't let go. You must bring him in. He got away from everyone else, but you are not letting him get away. But what am I going to tell my wife, if I even get to talk to her again? How long before someone pulls a gun and puts an end to me?*

While all this was happening—all the screaming and fighting—I looked up and saw an elderly woman holding a telephone receiver in her hand. She calmly looked at me and said, "I just called an ambulance. I think I'm having a heart attack." For all I know, that woman's call to 9-1-1 may have saved my life. I heard the police helicopter on the radio, attempting to find me.

"Uh, 77Fox, officer, just shine your light up at us, and we'll send in the troops."

"I can't! I'm inside the house, inside the door," I yelled back into the radio. Suddenly, the elderly woman opened the front door of the house to receive help from paramedics. A patrol car slowly moved by outside, and I shone my flashlight at it. Twenty thousand candlepower in the darkness is bright!

The patrol car stopped, and then another and another, until the house was swarming with officers. I managed to get Cheeks handcuffed, as well as the woman on my left. The woman who had been on my right managed to disappear and avoid arrest. I was treated by the paramedics for a cut on my left arm that ran from my wristwatch to beyond my elbow. Though it has faded some, I still carry that scar.

Now, what did I learn from this? There were a lot of police-type lessons to learn from the mistakes that both Duff and I made that night. But what were the important spiritual lessons?

One lesson that I believe God wanted me to learn on patrol that night is this. In the midst of the chaos, the day-to-day struggles of life, and the violence and corruption all around us, there is a voice within us that is calling us to shine our lights so that a rescue can take place. So many people need help and hope. We must shine our lights so that they may see their way to the cross of Christ. If you won't shine your light, then who will? Without the light, people perish.

"So that you will prove yourselves to be blameless and innocent, children of God above reproach in the midst of a crooked and perverse generation, among whom you appear as lights in the world" (Philippians 2:15 NASB). "Nor does anyone light a lamp and put it under a basket, but on the lampstand, and it gives light to all who are in the house" (Matthew 5:15–16).

Light overcomes darkness. When my flashlight beam blasted out of the house that night, it cut its way across the dark street and was easily visible to the responding officers. Where, only moments before, my beam of light had been blocked by the closed door of the house, it now drew the attention of those I desperately needed to come to my aid.

There are times when you and I are the ones who need assistance. We need someone's light to shine our direction, to provide wisdom in our decision-making, or perhaps to illuminate and expose sin that has crept in. Sadly, we too often allow our pride to keep us from asking for the help we need. I couldn't take Cheeks into custody all by myself that night, just as I cannot expect to successfully walk this Christian walk all alone.

Truthfully, neither can you. We need each other. We need the church. Shine your light for others, and ask for the help you need from your brothers and sisters when you need it.

Sixteen Days in July

"Therefore be careful how you walk, not as unwise men but as wise, making the most of your time, because the days are evil" (Ephesians 5:15–16).

How many days are we guaranteed in life? If you answered "none," then you are correct. We are promised many things in God's Word, but a certain number of days, weeks, or years is not one of them. By now, this should be a familiar question: what are you doing with the time God has given you?

It was July of 2001, and I was sitting in the lobby of the downtown public works building. I worked a four-hour, overtime security detail there every Thursday afternoon. For more than two years, the job had been extremely easy and, for the most part, uneventful. That was the way I liked it. On this particular hot day, I sat behind the information desk, trying to cool off after returning from changing a flat tire for a motorist in front of the building. It was 5:00 p.m.—only one hour to go.

From my position behind the desk, frantic movement caught my attention. I looked up to see a woman I recognized as a public works employee quickly approaching. Her face held a look of concern. I secretly hoped that she had returned for something she had forgotten, but she appeared to be heading directly toward me. Before I could ask her if she was okay, she blurted out, "There's a man on the bus who has had a heart attack. There's an officer doing CPR. Do we have an AED?"

An AED is an *automatic external defibrillator*, a small, portable device the size of a laptop computer. An AED is used to administer an electric shock to someone who has experienced a cardiac event, to restart his heart. I had received training in AED use, but it had been quite some time since I had completed that class.

I turned and opened the cabinet behind my chair, where the AED was kept. Immediately, a small alarm sounded, causing a number of heads in the lobby to snap around toward us. Removing the AED unit, I closed the cabinet and headed toward the front door. I instructed the woman who had reported the incident to return to the desk, call 9-1-1, and request that an ambulance be dispatched. Once outside, I quickly noticed a large, double-length commuter bus stopped against the curb, partially blocking the busy intersection. Heavy rush-hour traffic slowly crawled by, many of the drivers craning their necks to see what was happening on the corner.

I crossed the street, dodging a few of the rubbernecking motorists. A gathering crowd of onlookers watched the scene unfold. I turned left and saw a large man lying on his back on the sidewalk, as another officer performed chest compressions on him. My thoughts were clear, but I felt a brief moment of panic when I heard several people from the crowd say, "All right!" when I opened the AED unit. I wondered if I could remember how to use the thing, if I would be able to work the unit before it was too late. The man was turning blue, and I knew that he was in serious trouble. I attached the electrodes to the man's chest, according to the instructions, and told the other officer and a citizen to step back. In an instant, the AED unit failed to detect a heartbeat, and a mechanical voice spoke: "Shock recommended." I said, "Clear," and pushed the button.

Instantly, the large man's body seemed to lift off the sidewalk and return back down. His heart began to beat weakly. I looked to my left and noticed a number of passengers on the bus, watching anxiously, shocked at what they were witnessing. A marvel of modern technology seemed to be saving the day. An ambulance arrived and took over care of the man and transported him to a local hospital. When they arrived, I realized for the first time that one of the bus passengers I had seen watching in shock was the wife of the man. We would meet again.

When word got out that an AED unit had been successfully used, the news media and others began to pick up on the story. I was interviewed by a local television station and remembered a question asked of me: "Officer, how does it feel to be a hero? I mean, you saved this man's life."

I wanted so much to give God the glory for using me, so I responded, "God saved the man's life. I'm just glad that I was available to be used by Him." As the words left my mouth, I thought that my answer would certainly be deleted from the story and the broadcast. And I was right. It was deleted.

I was instructed by the department's media relations folks to dress up and appear at a press conference at the man's hospital on the following Tuesday morning. I showed up with my wife and met the man's wife, only to discover that we had all been members of the same Sunday school class nearly twenty years earlier. It is a small world, isn't it?

I was grateful to have been used by God to act as His hands in restoring life to this man, but I understand that God had done the work. I had simply been available for His use. I call this the doctrine of shared responsibilities. God does what only He can do, but He expects each of us to do the things He has equipped us to do. Remember the story of the feeding of the five thousand? Jesus worked the miracle, but

He used His disciples to organize the people and pass out the fish and bread.

The press conference ended, and I was asked if I wanted to go and see this man whose life I was credited with saving. I agreed, and with some nervous anticipation, I followed several others to his hospital room. How should I act? I didn't want to seem arrogant, like I was something special. I wanted to point to Christ, not to me.

I decided to play it cool. We arrived at the man's private hospital room and met his sister. The man had a trachea tube in and was not yet able to speak, but he could write. He looked at me and wrote something on a piece of paper and handed it to his sister. He took my hand in his and looked into my eyes, while she read the words, "I am alive." The man shook my hand and held on to it for a long time.

I had no idea what God was doing. I thought I did, as I often think I know what God is doing. I had been used by God before, as have so many of you, but somehow this was different. After that meeting, I returned to the hospital to give a copy of a media tape to the man. His words, "I am alive," repeated in my mind many times after the hospital visit.

Just over two weeks later, I received a telephone call informing me that the man had died. It seemed that he had been doing well, almost ready to be released to go home, but then he had begun to feel ill. He had returned to his hospital bed, and with his cardiologist standing there, he had simply died. His heart had stopped beating, and he was gone. Sixteen days after his heart attack, he was gone.

Now I was a bit confused. I wasn't angry with God, but I was not sure what had happened—not in terms of the surface story but deep down, in the spiritual realm. What had happened there? Why had God allowed me to become involved in this, to restart this man's heart, only for him die anyway? I didn't understand God's way in this situation.

My wife and I attended the memorial service, and there God gave me the answer I was searching for. I approached the man's wife, and as we hugged, I asked her what had happened, expressing my deep sympathy and sorrow.

Her response was surprising. I had expected her to be distraught and overwhelmed, but this was a woman of deep faith, whose hope and joy was found in her intimate relationship with Christ. She told me that her husband had been a wonderful man but that he had been a workaholic. In more than twenty years of marriage, he had never really shared his feelings, thoughts, or dreams with her. He had been emotionally distant. He rarely said "I love you," and he had never really expressed his pride in and love for their teenage son.

But in those sixteen days, given another chance, he had more than made up for all the lost time. She told me that those sixteen days meant more to her than many years of marriage before his heart attack. God had shown His great and boundless mercy in giving this man sixteen extra days to live. This entire experience hadn't been about me at all. It had been about the man on the bus.

Now, you might ask why God did not just totally heal the man, or why He even let the man have a heart attack at all. We often struggle with questions for which there seem to be no answers. The reason for the heart attack was easily traceable to the man's long-term health condition: too much work, too much food, and not enough exercise or rest. All these things contributed to bringing us to that moment on the sidewalk in downtown Houston in July 2001. But don't overlook the mercy of God in the midst of the tragedy: sixteen days, sixteen gifts to a wife and son.

Is there someone you can think of right now who needs to hear from you? Maybe your mother or father is longing to hear from you, to know that you are okay. Stop running. Maybe you've said some things to a friend or loved one that you regret, but you have let pride keep you from making the situation right. Husbands, are you withholding transparency and love from your wives? Wives, are you withholding honor or intimacy from your husbands? Remember why you fell in love in the first place, and rekindle the romance. Forgive one another for hurts and wrongs. Honor God, and love each other while you still can.

15

Danger and Overconfidence

"Two Adam twenty-three."

"2A23E, go ahead."

"Stand by, sir. 2A24E."

"2A24E."

"2A23E and 2A24E, check by with the narcotics unit at the central gas pumps. Code two."

"2A23E en route, ma'am."

"2A24E en route."

I was riding the evening shift out of the Central Patrol Station. Patrol units have characters in their unit numbers that provide information specific to that unit. For example, my unit, 2A23E, or "two Adam twenty-three E," told the police dispatcher a number of things particular to my assignment. The number two at the beginning designated the district to which I was assigned—out of some twenty-four districts into which the city was divided. The letter *A* (Adam) meant that I was assigned to the Central Patrol Station, as did the number two. Alpha characters were given to all patrol stations.

Central Patrol covered a large area of the city near the downtown central business district—districts one and two. District two was north of the station, and district one was to the south. The district was divided into five sub-districts called *beats*. The number "23" told the dispatcher that I was assigned to a "twenties" beat.

The "3" at the end of "23" meant that I was a late side unit. Each shift contained two schedules that overlapped each other by one hour. Early side evening shift ran from 2:00 p.m. until 10:00 p.m. and was given even numbers. Late side, which I rode, ran from 3:00 p.m. until 11:00 p.m. and was given odd numbers. The letter *E* simply designated me as an evening shift unit. This would only be important in the event that I worked a number of overtime hours. Then, when the night shift unit came on duty, there could be two units with the same number 2A23E and 2A23N. The way to tell them apart was the alpha character *D*, *E*, or *N*.

This seemingly insignificant information is important to the police dispatchers and officers working the streets. Officers who worked with a canine partner had unit designations with the letter *K* in the middle to identify themselves as a canine unit. Helicopters were called "Fox" units, and so on and so forth.

Let's get back to the current call for service. Plainclothes units, such as the narcotics unit we were dispatched to assist, often executed search or arrest warrants. They usually called the dispatcher over the air and simply requested that a patrol unit "check by" as they served a warrant, so as to have a uniformed presence on the scene and to provide transportation to jail in the event an arrest was made.

Officers who are young or new to the job are generally eager to check by and assist in serving those warrants. It is an exciting change of pace from running calls for service. Most officers found out quickly that this was also a very dangerous—and occasionally boring—thing to do. There could be a lot of waiting involved in executing a search or arrest warrant.

Most seasoned officers did not readily volunteer for these assignments. I had helped to serve a number of warrants over the years, and by this point in my career, I had found that sometimes the plainclothes unit's officers lacked important information. Some investigators knew precious little information about the physical location they were going to, and little to no information on who might be inside when they entered. Occasionally, the plainclothes officers themselves seemed unprepared for what they might encounter after a door was breached.

The difference here was that the other officer and I had been dispatched to assist. There had been no general radio request for volunteers to check by with the narcotics unit. We had been handpicked. This might have made some officers unhappy, but the other officer, who was nicknamed "Easy," and I had run a number of warrants with this particular narcotics unit. They knew us, and we knew them, and they trusted us not to do something stupid. Their sergeant, JR, was top-notch, professional, competent, and well-respected by the officers in his unit.

We met at the gas pumps beside the Central Police Station to go over the warrant information. We were given a chance to view the warrant and photos of any of the suspects we were after, and to meet the undercover (UC) officer. This was vitally important. A few years earlier, in a similar situation, the patrol officers had not been able to see who the UC officers were until they were in the midst of the warrant execution. Unfortunately, one UC officer had approached with gun in hand and without identifying clothing, and she had been mistaken for another drug suspect. On that day, she had been shot to death by a fellow officer who had ordered her to stop and drop her weapon. Things were done differently now, and Sergeant JR's narcotics squad was one of the best. We often either met with, or at least observed a photo of, the CI (citizen informant) as well.

Once all of this was done, we found out what time the deal was expected to go down and where we were to set up and wait. Sometimes we followed at a great distance in our marked patrol vehicle. When the deal was done, a "bust signal" would be given, and we all would rush in to affect the arrest and protect the UC officer. The bust signal could be something like removing a stick of chewing gum or cigarette pack from a pocket, a double tap of a car's brake lights, or any other prearranged signal. Sometimes we treated the UC officer like one of the crooks, so as not to blow his undercover status for future investigations in the same area, or even with the same suspect groups.

On this particular day, the narcotics squad placed the UC officer and the CI under surveillance and followed at a distance, switching tail cars every few miles, so as not to be detected by anyone in the target vehicle. Easy and I got into my patrol car and followed at a distance of more than a mile. We monitored the progress on a car-to-car radio channel, and after almost thirty minutes and many miles, we began to wonder where we were going. We were told to stop and wait a minute, until the squad could determine where the CI and UC officer were going. We stopped on the shoulder of the freeway and waited. Once they began to move again, we proceeded forward. At one point, someone in the narcotics squad gave us the wrong information. We were heading east down the freeway, when the radio transmission came across: "Okay, patrol, he's staying on the loop."

"Patrol clear."

"Patrol, okay, okay now. He just took 288 south, 288 south. You receive?"

"Patrol clear. Hang on, Easy," I said.

We had already passed the Highway 288 south exit ramp, and all I could do to keep from losing the narcotics squad was to make a new exit. I drove off the edge of the road and down the grassy hill, knocking a hole in the gas tank of the patrol car in the process. I pressed hard on the accelerator in order to reposition ourselves to where we needed to be.

We couldn't afford to fall too far behind. If the bust went down and there was not a marked unit, things could turn sour quickly. Sometimes, if there were uniformed officers or a marked unit at the scene, a crook would decide not to shoot it out or resist—not because we were so deadly, but because they realized that the undercover officers shouting "Police!" were, in fact, the real police.

It was dark outside by the time we arrived in a rural area unfamiliar to either Easy or me. We were told to find a place to hide for a while. Where could one hide a large blue-and-white car with a red, yellow, and blue light bar on top? At a church, that's where.

We found a church in the area and drove across the grassy churchyard to park behind the largest building available. Few crooks would be paying attention to a church building as they passed by, or so we hoped. We waited and listened to the car-to-car radio channel, getting updates on the progress of the investigation. On some of these assignments, we did some sitting and waiting, chomping at the bit for the bust signal to be given.

As we listened, we learned that the suspect's house was on a long, dead-end dirt road. This posed a little bit of a problem for us. Any suspects at the target house would observe us long before we could arrive and bail out of our car with our guns drawn. One of the rules of warrant execution that put things in our favor was the element of surprise. The other two were speed and force of action. In this setup, we might have none of the above. Nevertheless, we were professional, experienced, and ready! We felt certain that we could handle this situation, as we had proven ourselves in a number of other instances.

We listened, as the officers who had been following the UC officer's car were now hiding and watching the suspect's house. Cars carrying additional suspects had arrived at the house and had gone inside. Only the target suspect was supposed to be inside the house, but, as often happens in police work, things change, and you have to adapt quickly or suffer the consequences. As we listened, we felt tension rising. We could hear it in the voices of the officers talking to each other on the radio and occasionally providing us with an update. They had described to us the exterior of the target house, but now things were rapidly changing for the worse. We knew that we were now outnumbered, and somehow, for some reason, more cars of crooks were showing up. It must have been party night at the drug house.

Easy and I began to go over our own plan: how we would cover each other and where we would seek cover as we arrived at the target house. I checked to make sure my shotgun was loaded with as many rounds of three-inch, double-aught buckshot as I could stuff into it. Easy made some comment about wishing he had worn his body armor.

"305 to patrol," went the radio.

I answered them, "Patrol, go."

"Okay, dudes, when the bust signal goes down, haul butt and get there, 'cause this thing might turn into a bad deal real quick-like. There are at least twelve crooks at the house now. We don't have a clue who they are or what they are doing there, but there's a bunch of them."

"Patrol, clear."

Easy and I looked at each other with an I-wish-I-had-stayed-home-today look. We had run a lot of calls together over the years, and we knew this was beginning to sound like a bad situation. We were almost certain that a shoot-out was going to occur. I thought about my wife and kids back at home right then. I wondered again if this might be the night that I would not make it home. I wondered how they would react to the news if I should—

No time for that now. I needed to focus on the deal here, get ready, breathe, calm down, aim straight, and exit the car in a hurry. I hoped there would be a tree close by to use for cover. "Easy," I asked, "are you wearing your vest?" I was glad that I was wearing my own body armor—but then, I always wore my vest. I checked everything again. Yep, the shotgun was ready. Then we waited several more tense minutes.

"305 to all units: Forget it. We are calling this off. Repeat: the UC is outside, and he gave a signal. We are leaving. We will get them another night."

Whew! We were relieved, kind-of. There existed an emotional conflict between the relief we felt and our inflated egos telling us to man up and go anyway. We never would have admitted to Sergeant JR's squad or anyone else that we were okay with letting the crooks stay home that night, waiting to catch them another day.

Sometimes it's very hard to realize and admit that you are not prepared or equipped for the task at hand. It was wise to back off and wait until we, rather than the criminals, had the advantage. Rather than push a bad situation, the UC officer had called off the warrant execution temporarily. Giving the others in the house some excuse for leaving the party, he had exited the target house and met up with the squad. We would run the warrant another day.

We believed that we were prepared for almost anything, being well-trained, equipped, and experienced, but we also knew that we had entered an area where the bad guys had all the advantages.

Sergeant JR wasn't only good because he always got his man; he was good because he was smart and took care of his squad first.

In Matthew 7:14, Jesus called the gate small and the way narrow that lead to life. Those of us who are traveling that road must be aware of the dangers that exist just off the shoulder of the road. That night with the narcotics unit, we had before us a long, narrow road. The danger wasn't in the road itself, but in what waited for us off to the side. Off the road, it got dark, and in that darkness were quite a few people who didn't care for us at all. They had no respect for us or for what we stood for. In order to continue engaging in the drug trade, some of them would run at our arrival. Others would stand and fight. They would, if necessary, take our lives to protect their own.

Spiritually speaking, many hazards lie off the side of the straight and narrow road to heaven. So many times, as we travel that road, we believe that we are experienced and prepared, and we take the hazards too lightly. Because we are Christians, we think that the Devil and his crooks naturally fear us. We can allow our spiritual egos to overwhelm our common sense and good judgment. Believe me: they don't fear you. We can become overconfident in who we are and what we think we can do. Even Michael, the archangel, while in a dispute with the Devil, knew that power was not in himself but in the Lord (Jude v. 9).

Here, I believe, is the real danger. Anytime we place our confidence in our abilities, experiences, college degrees, titles, or anything or anyone other than Jesus Christ and His abilities and power, then we are walking into a battle that we are not likely to win. Perhaps you are counting on your own resourcefulness, goodness, wealth, or even the fact that you are a law enforcement officer to put you into God's good graces and guarantee your salvation, because you have a deal worked out with the "man upstairs." Because you are a member, officer, or pastor of a church, or because you perform charitable deeds, you may be confident that God will automatically open the door to heaven for you when you die.

Please, place no confidence in anything other than the salvation found in Jesus Christ. Your salvation and mine is based on the sacrificial, substitutionary death of Jesus Christ, and regardless of our professions, memberships, or degrees held, we must repent of our sins and be born again (John 3:3). Remember that Jesus began His public ministry calling for repentance (Matthew 4:17). The apostle Peter's sermon on the day of Pentecost demanded repentance (Acts 2:38). The apostle Paul clearly stated in Acts 17:30 that God declares that all men everywhere need to repent. Confidence in anything or anyone else is worthless.

16

The Welfare Check

One of the ways the police department organized the system of dispatching calls for service was to prioritize them. We did not use a ten-code, as some departments do, and as popularized on television programs. We simply called the situation what it was. Officers on the street had their own names for certain calls for service, and some of them cannot be printed here.

Our system was simple, and it worked like this. A citizen called the police to report, for example, a barking dog complaint and provided the call-taker with the pertinent information. The call-taker typed up a "call slip" with the information and sent it off to the appropriate police dispatcher. The dispatcher handling calls for service in that part of the city determined the appropriate beat patrol unit to assign the call to and then dispatched it.

In the old days, the police dispatchers were licensed police officers who were assigned to the Emergency

Communications Division for one reason or another. In more modern days, the police dispatchers are not police officers but highly trained civilian employees who work for the police department. A good dispatcher is treasured by the patrol officers.

Each call for service is prioritized according to how quickly the situation requires a police response. An emergency call for service, with lights and siren, was coded "priority one." A code two call was slightly less serious than a code one. Fascinating, right?

So, here's how the story went.

"2A23E."

"2A23E, go ahead, ma'am."

"2A23E, meet the unit at 2300 Airline Drive, Shadygrove Trailer Park, regarding a welfare check, code two."

"2A23E clear, en route."

There usually wasn't much information given over the radio for a code-two call, but we could typically find more detailed information on our in-car MDT. The MDT, mobile digital terminal, was a small computer inside the patrol car, which connected us, not only to the police dispatcher, but to state and national crime information centers. With just a push of some buttons on the MDT, we could run a "person's" check all across the country for outstanding warrants or a valid driver's license. We could also talk to other officers over the computer rather than the radio, leaving the air uncluttered for emergency communications.

Nothing was more frustrating than to grab one's radio microphone during an emergency and be unable to broadcast because some knucklehead was talking about unimportant information that could have been relayed over the computer.

I was a field-training officer (FTO) at this time, and I had a fairly new female rookie riding with me. We arrived at the listed location and were met by another uniformed officer, who was sitting in his patrol car at the entrance to the trailer park. He told us that his mother had called to report that his uncle had threatened suicide. With the permission of his immediate supervisor, this officer could travel into our area to check on his uncle, but only if he had a beat unit backing him up. We were the backup unit. We asked the usual things that might become important to us later, such as: did he live alone, did he have any weapons inside the trailer, was he taking medications, had he ever done this before, etc.

We followed the other officer down a winding, narrow road in the trailer park, and he came to stop directly in front of his uncle's trailer house. We immediately felt uneasy about this. Parking in front of the door made us sitting ducks, especially if the suicidal uncle decided he really did want to take his own life—and didn't care to go alone. Perhaps the officer's familiarity with his uncle caused him to fail to recognize the potential for danger. Familiarity and apathy can be an officer's worst enemy. I placed our car in reverse and backed to where we could at least have some cover as we approached the front door.

It was dark outside. A surrealistic quiet hovered over the area. I allowed the other officer to take the lead, since he was, after all, the primary unit and family member of the uncle who lived in the trailer. As we stepped up onto the small front porch, my rookie was behind me. We listened for any sounds coming from inside the trailer, as we prepared to knock on the door. I motioned to my rookie to stand to the side, as the other officer knocked on the door. When he received no response from inside the trailer, he knocked harder. Still, no response came from within the house.

We began to walk slowly around the trailer, trying to peek in through the windows. The funny thing about a trailer house is that, once you step off the front porch, they are really tall. On our tiptoes, we still couldn't see into the windows, so we regrouped at the porch to decide on plan B. We called for a district supervisor over the radio, explained our situation, and requested permission to force entry into the house. Because a life was in danger, we were given permission to enter without a warrant. The other officer used his heavy police flashlight to knock the little window out of the front door. The idea was to reach inside and unlock the door so we could get in to check on his uncle.

As soon as the window broke, smoke poured out of the opening. No words were necessary for each of us to understand the seriousness of the situation we faced—and the necessity to act quickly. Single-wide trailer houses are notorious for burning down rapidly, and time was something that was not on our side at this point. Reaching in through the broken window, the other officer fumbled around until he found the door lock, and with a twist or two, we were inside.

Have you ever seen those television shows where the hero runs into a burning building without an oxygen mask or any protection, looks around for the victim, and brings him out unscathed? Those programs are not only fake, but dangerously unrealistic. More people die from smoke inhalation than from flames, and as we entered the trailer, all kinds of scenarios were running through my mind.

Seeing was very difficult, and breathing was no better. My eyes were burning, causing me to blink rapidly, seeking relief. My mind raced with the real possibility that there was an armed, suicidal man in there somewhere, and it was as frightful a situation as any I had faced before. With all our senses straining to work properly in the thickening smoke, we tried to move rapidly to locate the suicidal man before he located us. "Here he is, on the couch," I heard a stressed voice shout through gasps for clean air.

There on the sofa, facedown, was a man in his mid-fifties. The couch was a smoldering mess, and I believed that it would burst into flames any second. We reached out, and each of us grabbed any part of the man we could, dragging him toward the open door and fresh air. Several prescription pill bottles were on the burning sofa beside the man. I snatched them up.

I gasped for air. I needed air, and I needed it now—and without a hint of smoke, thank you very much. Back outside, we deposited one unconscious, limp human being on the porch deck. We were gasping for air, choking and dry-heaving. It was bad, to say the least, but our work wasn't done. Once we had quickly determined that the man was still breathing shallow breaths and had a pulse, we returned to the interior of the trailer, searching for anyone else who might be in there. We had already called for the fire department, but rather than wait, I grabbed a fire extinguisher from the trunk of our patrol car, and we went back into the trailer house to put out the still smoky, smoldering fire. The fact that it had not yet completely erupted into killing flames could only be attributed to God's mercy.

Now, here were three people risking their lives to save the life of someone who really didn't want to live any longer. Does that make sense to you? One officer was related to the man who wanted to die, so perhaps he felt a family obligation to make the attempt to rescue the dying man. But what about the other two of us? What did we have to gain by being burned or suffering from all the toxic smoke we inhaled that night? Jesus said, "Greater love has no one than this, that one lay down his life for his friends" (John 15:13

NASB). Okay, but we weren't friends with the suicidal man, were we?

After his medical recovery and some psychological help, the previously suicidal man became very grateful for what we had done for him that night. He wrote a thank-you letter to us that was quite touching.

This story reminds me of the parable of the good Samaritan found in Luke 10:30. As Jesus concluded the story, He asked His listeners this question: "Who was the neighbor to the man who had fallen among thieves?" There may be times when God literally expects us to lay down our lives for someone else. Fortunately, most of the time when He tells us to lay down our lives, He isn't talking about our physical death. Daily, we are to set aside *our* will in order to do *His* will (Matthew 16:24). More often than not, it seems that we do our own thing and then ask God to bless it.

To whom are you being a neighbor? No one lives his life only to himself, without responsibility toward others. Each of us has ample opportunity to positively impact the lives of others by being a neighbor—whether it's to a family member or a complete stranger. I challenge you to conduct a few welfare checks of your own this week. Pray, seek the Lord, and take up your cross as you head out on patrol.

17

Compassion

It was a terrible scene, but nothing I hadn't seen numerous times before. In fact, I had seen much more gruesome things than this. It wasn't a particularly gory scene that had grabbed my attention. What had me glued to the scene before me could perhaps be described as morbid fascination. When a two-thousand-plus-pound automobile collides with a piece of wood, namely an oak tree, the results are often mind-boggling. But it wasn't the twisted remains of what used to be a shiny car that stopped me in my tracks. It was what I saw inside the twisted remains.

I quickly counted the bodies inside the car: one up front and two in the backseat area. Three teenage bodies had been tossed around the car interior like life-size rag dolls. One of these in particular drew my attention. She really appeared to be sleeping, and if not for the fact that she was upside down in the backseat of the twisted vehicle, she would have appeared to be rather peaceful. I had seen people in much worse condition survive car wrecks, shootings, stabbings, dog bites, etc. There had been times when I felt that people were certainly a second away from eternity, and they ultimately made complete recoveries.

I was not the primary unit on this scene, so I was somewhat uncommitted initially. As I stood in the street, looking over the scene, a shout from one of the paramedics brought me back to reality. "Hey, give me a hand, would ya?"

I turned to see that the young girl had been removed from the wreckage, and the paramedic was beginning CPR. I quickly knelt down and took over the Ambu bag, forcing air into her lungs. People scurried around us, and work began on the second backseat passenger, a teenage boy. The driver was still in the wrecked car, semiconscious, moaning in pain. I focused on the work assigned me—to breath for this young lady, slowly, rhythmically. I worked the bag, forcing air into her lungs, letting the bag refill with air, squeezing again to push more air into her lungs. I spoke to her as I continued to work the bag, not sure that she could hear my words of encouragement.

The paramedic worked quickly to start an IV. As I worked, I looked at the young lady's face and hair. I noticed the earrings she was wearing, the clothes she had on. I wondered if somewhere that night, at that very moment, her mother and father might be sitting near a window of their home, waiting for her return. I wondered if perhaps they might be looking for the headlights of the car she had left in that night, signaling that their daughter was home safe. I wondered if they knew. Did they feel it? Did they somehow know that something was wrong, that their girl was injured? Would someone have to make a visit to their home that night to give them the bad news? Would it be me?

I determined to chase away those thoughts for now. I was a professional, after all. I had seen dozens of victims of crime or traffic accidents before. I had not let any of it bother me in years. What was going on here? I told myself silently not to allow this carnage to affect me, to simply look at this as a scene to be worked, an assignment to be accomplished. I prayed, "God, please, please let me help this girl. Please, Lord, put breath back into her lungs, and keep her heart beating. Please!"

Was that fair of me to ask God for this? After all, He hadn't put that young lady there, lying in the street with a broken neck and numerous internal injuries. God had not caused the car she was riding in to speed out of control past the convention center that night. God had not planted the tree that the car had struck. And God was not the one who had failed to buckle up a seat belt.

All of those choices had been made by the young lady and the two friends with whom she'd been riding. All of them knew the dangers of driving too fast, not wearing a seat belt, and mixing driving with alcohol and drugs. They knew! We all know these things. As sad as the situation was, they had known better. They had been told. Knowing these facts, however, did not take away the sorrow or pain involved in a preventable incident such as this.

Speed limit signs were posted. Traffic lanes were clearly marked. The bend in the road was obvious, signs alerting motorists were present, and the street was well lit.

Some people might look at that scene and the loss of young lives and ask why someone hadn't done something to prevent it. Why hadn't a cop been there to stop them before they sped into that tree? Why had someone from the parks department planted that tree at that location in the first place? Why didn't the car have an air bag, or if it did, why didn't it deploy? Why, why, why? In our attempts to ease our pain, we seek answers to questions that may never be answered to our satisfaction. We may seek to place blame in order to find understanding. The question of *why* is usually the first question asked as a part of the grieving process, and it is often the last question answered.

In the spiritual realm, it is much the same. Some people travel the road of life like a car filled with carefree teenagers. Most do not even realize that they are speeding out of control, until they hit the tree. Like spiritual cops, there are warnings all around us. Why don't people listen?

Maybe the cop is the church pastor. Each and every week, he preaches sermons, warnings, and exhortations, but some people don't heed them. I've heard people complain that the preacher is always yelling at them. "Why is the preacher so angry?" they ask. "I don't like a preacher who's always yelling. If I wanted to be yelled at, I could just stay at home."

Maybe the cop is your spouse. "Nag, nag, nag. That's all she ever does." "That husband of mine just thinks I am too stupid to do anything on my own. He's so bossy and oppressive, I'll show him." So, just for a second or two, you take your hands off the wheel and your eyes off the road. Now, that wasn't so bad. Nothing happened. So you do it again. Hey, this danger is kind of addictive and rather exciting, isn't it? And then you crash. Maybe it's just a fender bender and not a fatal wreck—at least, it's not physically fatal.

As in the days of the prophet Jeremiah, God tries to reach us today. Jeremiah 6:10 (NASB) puts it this way: "To whom shall I speak and give warning that they may hear? Behold, their ears are closed and they cannot listen. Behold, the word of the LORD has become a reproach to them; they have no delight in it."

You may be a police officer yourself, and God has been trying to reach you, to warn you. If you are not listening, if you are failing to maintain your officer safety or are near to compromising your ethics, professionalism, morals, or marriage vows, if you are bowing to the peer pressure of the job, then you are about to hit the oak tree. Before it is too late and you have left the roadway, bring things back under control. Talk to someone who will help you and hold you accountable. Compromise may end your marriage or career. When taking the oath of office, no police officer ever expects to end up in prison, but it has happened countless times. Take God with you fully when you go on patrol.

18

BEAR ONE ANOTHER'S BURDENS

I always liked working the late side evening shift because it was almost a normal schedule. Working 3:00 p.m. until 11:00 p.m. gave me the entire morning to do things before going to work, and it allowed me to get home early enough at night to get some sleep. It did, however, cause me to miss many important times in the lives of my small children.

The shift started out being busy enough to keep things interesting, and it turned even busier as it wound down. The down side to this was that I frequently received a late call, which meant that I wasn't going home until the wee morning hours of the following day. I received some unusual late calls during my time on the streets, but this chapter is devoted to an early call.

It was a typical, hot summer afternoon in district two, Houston's Near Northside. District two also included an old neighborhood known as The Heights.

For several weeks, there had been reports of a male exposer along the Whiteoak Drive bayou jogging trail. Houston isn't called the Bayou City without reason. The Whiteoak Drive jogging trail paralleled Whiteoak Bayou for several miles, weaving in and out of a wooded area that grew between the bayou and Whiteoak Drive. At times, the jogging trail ran near the bayou, and at other locations, it turned away from the bayou and curved through the woods to reappear nearer to the street than to the bayou. During an earlier period, the locally infamous "Beer Belly Rapist" had used the woods along Whiteoak Bayou as his staging area for attacking female joggers.

Our concern with the increasing number of exposer reports was that the suspect was becoming increasingly bold in approaching his victims. There existed a real concern that at some point, exposing himself would no longer be enough for him, and he would progress into physical confrontations with joggers. When time allowed—between calls for service—patrol units in the area would drive slowly along Whiteoak Drive in the hope than an increased police presence would discourage the culprit. I refer to this tactic as "LYPBK," which means "letting your presence be known," something I had been taught years earlier by a veteran officer. It is an effort to be visible and be available to citizens in case something happens.

One afternoon, shortly after leaving the evening shift roll call, another evening shift unit broke the air and alerted the dispatcher that they were engaged in a foot pursuit along Whiteoak Bayou. The description of the suspect they were after fit the description of the flasher who frequented the Whiteoak jogging trail. I immediately notified the dispatcher that I was en route to the location. As I arrived and began trying to determine exactly where the primary unit was, I slowed my patrol car, drove over the curb, and proceeded through the grassy area near the jogging trail. My patrol car straddled the jogging trail as I slowly drove west.

After I had gone a short distance, a uniformed officer stepped out from behind some trees, waving his arms to get my attention. I threw my car into park, turned off the ignition, and bailed out. The officer who had flagged me down directed me to follow him into the woods. The woods quickly opened up to reveal a small pond that had been created by a recent overflow of the bayou from heavy rains. When the flood waters had receded, a naturally low area had retained water. It was filled with trash and debris, not to mention snakes and nasty, biting mosquitoes.

While the flood zone pond was not a surprise, what stood in the center of the pond was. Right smack-dab in the middle of this particular pond was a very large man in waist-deep water. On the bank of the pond opposite me, I noticed a rookie officer still in full uniform, soaking wet. He had fallen in, he said, while chasing the exposer suspect.

By this time, several more patrol units had arrived on scene, having responded to the foot chase broadcast by the primary unit. Somehow, we needed to get the suspect out of the water and into custody. He was going to be charged with at least one count of indecent exposure for what he had been doing when the foot chase began. How to get him out of the water was the big question of the day.

Let me share a secret with you. Most police officers do not like to get dirty. They don't want to get anything on their uniforms, hands, shoes, or anything else, and for good reason. Not only do officers pay their own cleaning bills, but the potential for contracting illness or injury is a very real concern. So, we had a predicament here, didn't we?

A district two patrol supervisor—nicknamed "Taser Tom" for his frequent use of a conducted energy device (CED), commonly referred to as a *Taser*—arrived on scene and put his brain to work. "Let's call the dive team and see if they will bring a boat out here." We tried to arrange it, but the dive team said no, they didn't respond to calls of that sort. So Taser Tom, true to his nickname, stepped to the edge of the pond, stretched his arm toward the suspect in the water, aimed his CED more or less in the suspect's direction, and fired. With a bang, the little barbs shot out toward the suspect, but when they reached the end of their connecting wires, they dropped straight down into the water with a tiny splash—way short of the suspect.

The firing of the CED seemed only to cause the suspect in the water to become agitated. He began to shout all kinds of odd things, the most memorable being his claim: "I'm Michael Jackson! I'm Michael Jackson!" Taser Tom threw a stick at him and yelled, "Shut up, Michael!" The stick fell as short of the intended target as the CED darts had. It was all we could do to keep from falling in the water with laughter.

Time was ticking away. It was hot outside. The suspect was still in the water, yelling at us and tossing pieces of wood, Coke bottles, or whatever floated by him, in our general direction. It was time for Taser Tom to earn his supervisor's pay and make a command decision. "You go in and get him," said Taser Tom, pointing at the still dry senior officer from the original unit.

"You ... uh ... you want me to go in there?" asked the officer, pointing at the dirty pool.

"That's right. You're the primary unit. Go and get him out of there," Taser Tom ordered.

There was a slight pause in the action at this point, as the officer processed just what he was being ordered to do. Nevertheless, he unhooked his gun belt and handed it to another officer standing nearby. As he began to remove his uniform shirt and body armor, another officer and I looked at each other and began to remove our gun belts also. Taser Tom asked us what we were doing. I responded, "That crook will drown him if he goes in there alone. We're going with him."

We hung our nice blue uniform shirts and gun belts on tree limbs, emptied our wallets and other items from our pants pockets, and slowly walked toward the edge of the water. I had gingerly moved into the water a few steps, trying not to slip in the mud, when my breath disappeared for a moment. I wondered how the water could feel so cold on such a hot day? I prayed that the water was too cold for snakes. As we slowly waded toward the crook, stumbling over unseen, submerged debris, he began shifting around nervously in the water, as if he was seeking a way of escape. By this time, I realized that the suspect's appearance was seriously misleading. While he appeared to be standing in water that was no more than three feet deep, we were already chest-deep in the stinking, debris-filled water, and we were still yards away from where he stood.

As we neared the suspect, he stepped off of whatever had been holding him up. We were all neck-deep in the water now. Upon reaching the suspect, who was trying his best to do the backstroke away from us, the primary unit officer reached out to grab hold of him. The crook did just as I had predicted and pushed the officer under the water. I was close by, doing something like a doggy paddle and occasionally touching a foot on the muddy bottom of the pond. I reached out and gave the crook a solid punch to the chin with my right fist. His head moved back a bit, and he released his grip on the officer he was trying to drown. Then he fixed his wild eyes on me. *Oops,* I thought. *Maybe I should have hit him harder.*

Now there were four of us in the water. After much effort, we managed to drag the crook close enough to the water's edge for Taser Tom to dart him with the remaining CED round. I'm not sure if it worked as it was designed to, but we did finally manage to roll the man onto the bank of the pond, where he was properly handcuffed and searched. Exhausted and filthy, we all retrieved our uniform parts from the surrounding tree limbs and placed them into our patrol cars.

After a trip to a local hospital for a checkup because of our exposure to the nasty water, we completed the paperwork on the suspect. One of the officers had an apartment nearby, and he offered me a change of clothes until we could finish up and head home. I accepted his kind offer, but I was a bit surprised when he handed me a pair of baggy, multicolored pants, a T-shirt, and matching flip-flop sandals. Every other officer I passed stared for a moment before exploding in laughter.

Okay, so what's the point to all of this? I believe there are at least two lessons to be learned.

The first lesson has to do with our need for each other's support in the Christian life. When Taser Tom ordered the officer to go in and get the crook out of the water, he was talking only to the one officer. The order was given, and the officer intended to follow it to the best of his ability, but the burden placed upon him was too great to handle alone. He would try his best, but there was a really good chance that, without help, he would drown in the process.

There exists an individual responsibility to the Lord's commands, and each believer will be held responsible (2 Corinthians 5:10). However, we are called to support one another and even to bear one another's burdens (Galatians 6:2).

Our footing in this life can seem muddy, slippery, and shifting, especially as our society moves further away from traditional church values and beliefs. With all of the murkiness and debris, we can hardly see where we are stepping. Knowing what to believe can be confusing. The waters are much deeper than they appear, and when you wade off into them alone, you can quickly find yourself in over your head. You may have been caught off guard by trouble or temptation that you did not see coming.

Whatever the situation, the principle of restoration and bearing the burdens of others found in Galatians 6 applies to more situations than just being caught in sin. We often either ignore the faults of another or judge too harshly. It is apparent that we all have burdens, and God commands us to bear them together.

The second lesson has become more obvious to me after some experience in the pastorate. Far too many believers are content to stand on the banks of the pond and watch someone else wade into the battle. Few churchgoers ever obey the Lord's command, found in Mark 16:15, to preach the gospel. The word for *preach* is a verb that literally means "to proclaim in the manner of a herald." In other words, we are to shout the gospel out for people to hear.

Somehow, over the years, believers have come to identify the Great Commission as the responsibility of church pastors. Many feel that inviting their lost family and friends to church fulfills the Great Commission. If they just get them to show up for "Friend Day," the pastor will preach to them.

Obey the Lord, and take over your pastor's burden by heralding the good news of Jesus.

19

THE DEVIL IS REAL

The southwest side of Houston is large and heavily populated. When I was a kid growing up in the near southwest area, I could walk barefoot to the corner store, approximately eight blocks from my parents' home. I recall walking with my friends along any number of local bayous and alleyways, looking for glass bottles. We collected all the glass bottles we could find, and if they were the right kind, we took them to the corner store for the deposit money. We would then buy whatever we could with the money we had received for the deposits. We were being "green" before the term was popularized.

Years later, when I was a new police officer, my first patrol assignment was in the same neighborhood where I had grown up. As a police officer, I was surprised to see how much crime and trouble existed on those same streets where I had walked barefoot as a child. I wondered whether the neighborhood had actually changed that much, or if my job had made me aware of the realities of the area. I believe it was a combination of both.

Not much was going on as I drove the patrol car through a strip center near my childhood home. The rookie officer with me was more bored than I was, but we perked up upon hearing the dispatcher's voice over the radio. She dispatched us to a call regarding a suspicious man in the traffic lanes of Bellaire Boulevard, a major surface street in the area. It didn't take much work to locate him.

We parked in a parking lot near the suspicious man, who turned out to be much younger than expected. While I have forgotten his name, the encounter has never left me. The young man was an African-American teenager, around seventeen years of age. The first thing about him that seemed out-of-place was the winter coat he was wearing in the heat of a summer evening. He was covered in sweat, and panic and fear covered his face. We approached him cautiously and began by asking him to step out of the street. The young man was very cooperative and polite. We attempted to determine his identity and his reason for being in the street. His story was a peculiar one.

"Yes, sir, I am out here on a mission, sir," he said militarily.

"And what mission would that be?" I asked.

"I am here to kill the Devil, sir." He spoke to us as if he was a soldier—very polite and straightforward, always ending his sentences with "sir."

"Kill the Devil. What are you talking about?" asked the rookie.

"Sir, the Devil is bad, and I must kill him to stop him from doing evil things."

"Okay, now tell me this. How do you intend to kill the Devil, and just where is he right now?" was my follow-up question.

"Sir, the Devil is underground, under the streets, and all these people are in danger. I have to get under the street, sir."

This was getting strange. We needed to find out who this kid was and where he belonged. I couldn't help but think that he must have family somewhere, looking for him. While we waited for the dispatcher to check the missing persons reports for the day, we continued to talk to the young man. I said, "So, tell me how you get under the street to find the Devil."

"Sir, you know those manhole covers? Well, I find one where the Devil is hiding, and I use my superhuman strength to lift the cover and jump down in there." At this point, the young man became very emotional and began crying, wailing, sobbing. Somehow, in his disturbed mind, he felt on his shoulders the entire weight of protecting the human race. He felt that if he did not find and defeat the Devil, many lives would be lost, and the strain of that thought was too much to bear. His already fragile mental state seemed to break under the strain, and it took some time to bring him back under control, though reality still seemed to elude him.

We loaded him into the patrol car, and he was able to direct us to his home, where we released him to his family. We had successfully handled the call for service, but I couldn't forget this young man. This incident occurred years before the development of crisis intervention programs that assisted officers in their understanding and handling of situations involving mentally ill people.

Was this young man really mentally disturbed? Yes, I think we could say that he was, and yet his belief wasn't too far from reality. According to numerous Scriptures, the Devil is quite real, powerful and dangerous. In the book of James we find an often partially quoted passage: "Submit therefore to God. Resist the Devil and he will flee from you" (James 4:7 NASB). I say that it is often *partially* quoted because too often we only repeat the part about resisting the Devil and his flight from us.

The prerequisite to resisting the Devil, which means standing against him, is submission to God. Only then can we resist. Unless you have submitted yourself to God, your attempts at resisting the Devil will be fought in your own strength alone, and you will fail. Our greatest struggle seems to be in submitting to God, the very thing that puts us in position to resist evil.

Like the young man that night, some believers think that they can defeat the Devil in their own superhuman strength. They may even proudly say that they "rebuke the Devil" or "cast him out of our church services" or "plead the blood of Jesus over a situation"—actions that are neither found in nor commanded of us in Scripture. Such claims are all about the people who make them, and except for ending a prayer "in Jesus' name," they may exclude God altogether. Without submission to God's authority, we cannot even discern the important spiritual battle lines clearly enough to keep us from wandering aimlessly into enemy territory.

What is missing from the practices of many modern-day churches is *obedience*. Obedience has become a four-letter word to many who attempt to make God's grace into a get-out-of-jail-free card, where no one bears any responsibility to obey God. This is not necessarily only a modern practice, as Jesus Himself asked, "Why do you call Me, 'Lord, Lord,' and do not do what I say?" (Luke 6:46 NASB).

James 4:7–8 holds great promise for believers. We don't have to defeat the Devil. We must simply resist him after submitting to God. Jesus won the victory on the cross.

20

Who Will Stand Up?

There is an unspoken practice among patrol officers that you do not issue a citation to or arrest a doctor or a nurse unless you absolutely have to. The reasoning behind this unofficial "rule" is that you never know when you might be injured and in need of medical care. You don't want to look up from a hospital gurney to see the nurse or doctor you cited looking down at you. This practice is perhaps based more in superstition than anything.

On the night shift, things usually began to pick up right around 2:00 a.m., when state law required bars to close. This was a dangerous time to be on the street. Intoxicated drivers were headed somewhere, and it seemed that most accidents involving alcohol occurred after 2:00 a.m. I was slowly driving through the parking lot of a nightclub called The Rodeo, a country and western dance hall saloon, just before closing time. A lot of the patrons of the bar were men, mostly urban cowboys with large pickup trucks and equally large hats. I had more than one high-speed chase begin at the parking lot exit of the The Rodeo.

While slowly cruising the parking lot, I noticed a small, green car pull out of the parking lot onto N. Gessner Street. The car drove over the curb onto the grassy median separating the northbound and southbound lanes and then continued another fifty feet before reentering the main traffic lanes. Figuring that something was wrong with the driver or the vehicle, I pulled in behind the car and initiated a traffic stop.

The car turned left and continued through the drive-through lane of a fast-food restaurant, finally stopping behind the business where the parking lot ended. I exited my patrol car and approached the driver's door of the little green car. Before I could say a word, the car door opened, and a young woman swung her legs outside of the car and looked up at me. "Can you help me?" she asked. "I've had way too much to drink." Oh yeah, I could help her, certainly, no problem at all. I could help her take a breathalyzer test, help her to be booked into the city jail, and help her have her car towed to an impound lot.

What is your experience with intoxicated motorists? In my experience, this is the most preventable crime that occurs in every city, county, or state—and one that costs many innocent lives each year.

This wasn't the first person I had arrested for driving intoxicated, nor would it be the last. However, this case would become quite interesting in court.

In those days, a person suspected of driving while intoxicated (DWI) was taken to the downtown police complex at 61 Riesner Street. This address included the Central Patrol Station, the jail, many administrative offices, and the room we simply referred to as "Intox." Intox housed interview rooms in which suspects were videotaped, as well as the devices for testing breath alcohol content. The suspect was provided an opportunity to complete what is commonly referred to as a "field sobriety test." When this occurred at the location of the traffic incident, local attorneys who specialized in defending DWI charges called it "roadside gymnastics."

In this case, during the videotaped portion, the suspect insisted on calling her lawyer, which turned out to be her uncle. She also took the breath test, and the results, as I recall, indicated that she was indeed above the legal limit, at the time, of 0.1% blood alcohol content. Today's legal limit is set at 0.08%.

After her arrest and while I was completing paperwork, I found out that the young lady was a nurse at a local hospital. Unfortunately for her, the fact that she was a nurse was not going to prevent her from being charged with driving while intoxicated. Several of my coworkers questioned me about why I would arrest a nurse. They reasoned that she might work on me someday, if I was ever injured in the line of duty, and they asked why I had not called a taxi cab to take her home. *Thanks for the support, guys,* I thought.

At her trial, her lawyer/uncle had me draw on a chalkboard a picture of the scene where I had first observed his defendant, and where she had stopped her car. Then he began a series of questions intended to discredit my probable cause for conducting the traffic stop. If he could remove the probable cause for the stop, then the defendant could certainly be released with charges dropped or a not-guilty finding by the jury.

The defense attorney waited until I was reseated in the witness box and then continued his questioning. "Officer Caronna, could you tell the jury the turning radius of a Volkswagen Quantum?" I'm not sure who looked more surprised at the question—the jury, the prosecutor, or me.

"No, sir, I can't." I was thinking about what a stupid question that was. Of course, the lawyer knew the answer and told it to the jury.

Then he proceeded. "Now, Officer Caronna, isn't it possible that the reason my client's car drove over the curb was really due to the car's turning radius and the narrow street, and that there simply is no way to avoid the curb?" I found his reasoning ridiculous.

"No, sir. That isn't true at all. I've seen a number of eighteen-wheelers exit the parking lot at the same driveway and make the turn without so much as touching the curb." Point for the prosecution?

His strategy wasn't working well, so he switched gears, trying to play on the sympathy of the jury. "Officer Caronna, did you know that my client is a nurse?"

"Not when I arrested her, no, sir. I learned that after she had been arrested."

"Did you know that her uncle was a lawyer?"

"No, sir, I didn't know that either."

Where was this guy going with his questions? And where is this chapter going?

Let me ask you a question. Do you have convictions? No, not convictions for criminal offenses; I'm referring to things you believe in strongly. Do you believe the Scriptures? Have you ever sworn an oath or given your word on something—like wedding vows, perhaps? If so, you'd better keep your word.

My point here is that I had sworn an oath of office back in early 1983 when I graduated from the police academy. Part of that oath was, as I have already stated, to enforce the laws of the land. Sometimes following the oath wasn't pleasant, but then most of the job was unpleasant. Yes, the defendant was a nurse and was likely was very good at her job. However, her status as a nurse was not the issue here. It was her status as an intoxicated motorist that had brought us to trial. The trial was declared a mistrial, because the jury felt compassion over the woman's status as a nurse. The charge was refiled by the district attorney's office. However, the woman pled guilty in order to avoid another costly trial, stay out of jail, and keep her driver's license.

The case reminded me that Christians are to uphold the laws of God's Word. We do that by speaking the truth, no matter the cost. No matter what is the popular thing to do, we stand up for what is right, and we oppose what is wrong or unjust. We defend the defenseless, and even if coworkers or fellow believers compromise themselves, we stand strong. We walk the difficult, narrow road, and there are times when it seems that even those who should be encouraging us to press on are pointing us to an early exit ramp.

I believe that God is still looking for those who will stand up and do the right thing without regard for the cost. The lost world could really use people who are genuine in their pursuit of Jesus, people who stand for the truth and are not concerned with political correctness. "Who will stand up for me against evildoers? Who will take his stand for me against those who do wickedness?" (Psalm 94:16).

"Wickedness" may seem a harsh word to apply to an intoxicated driver. The word translates as "trouble" or "sorrow" as well as "idolatry." Many of us have experienced the trouble and sorrow that intoxicated drivers cause for themselves and others. Moreover, it can be argued that placing one's desire to drink and drive over the interest and safety of others is the worship of oneself.

Will you stand up for God? Whatever situation you find yourself facing—in your job, your church, or your family—will you stand up? It may cost you status, or worse, but remember the promise of Jesus found in Mark 10:29–30 "Jesus said, "Truly I say to you, there is no one who has left house or brothers or sisters or mother or father or children or farms, for My sake and for the gospel's sake, but that he will receive a hundred times as much now in the present age, houses and brothers and sisters and mothers and children and farms, along with persecutions; and in the age to come, eternal life."

All that you sacrifice for Him or for the sake of the gospel will be returned to you many times over.

21

WITHOUT NATURAL AFFECTION

When I was still a new believer, I was asked why I was so intent on reading the Bible and talking about religious stuff. "Because Jesus is coming back soon," was my response. The reply I received was that men had been saying that for years and years, and nothing had changed. No, Jesus has not yet returned as promised, but He will, and I believe it could be soon.

I heard the emergency tone beep over the police radio. I wondered who was about to be dispatched for what emergency and where it would be. Most officers kind of cringed when they heard that tone, especially if it was late in their shift or time for a meal. Most officers didn't want a code-one call when it was almost time to go home or to an extra job.

"Two Adam twenty-three," came the dispatcher's voice.

Oh man, it was for me. "Twenty-three go," I shot back in a rather grumpy voice.

"Two Adam twenty-three, I have a shooting that just occurred at Airline Drive and West Cavalcade, no other information. Code one."

"Clear," I snapped. I wasn't far from that location, and as I flipped the switch to activate the car's emergency lights and siren, I pictured the intersection in my mind.

As I sped along with backup units en route, I tried to imagine what was at that intersection and what I might find when I arrived. I could not think of a single place of business, residence, or even a cardboard box that stood there. I had already asked the dispatcher to try the call-back number for more detailed information, hoping to learn something before I arrived. But it was too late. I was already there, and so was a fire department ambulance.

The commotion seemed to be centered on the southeast corner of the intersection. Just as I'd thought, nothing stood on that corner except for a faded billboard. The corner was mostly patches of weeds, with a dirt trail worn deep from the many feet that had plodded around the corner and up Airline Drive for years, where no sidewalk had ever been paved.

I exited the car quickly and found the paramedics working on a young boy. He appeared to be around twelve years of age and had been shot a number of times by someone who had fled the scene. As the shooting victim was loaded into the ambulance and transported to a local trauma center, I noticed another young boy on a bicycle. In fact, this boy was sitting on one bicycle while holding on to another—the victim's bicycle—by the handlebars. He appeared to be in shock. Memories of riding bikes with friends during my childhood quickly flashed in and back out of my mind. I began my investigation. What I learned didn't make sense to me.

Both boys had spent the past few hours at the Boys and Girls Club of Houston, where they went every day after school. There they participated in team sports and other recreational activities intended to keep kids off the streets and out of trouble. Trouble had found them anyway, and I needed to find out why and by whom.

In Exodus 20, God told His people not to commit murder. He just said, "Don't do it." A child had been murdered here, and I was astounded when I found out why this young boy had been shot. He hadn't been dealing drugs, involved in the robbery of a local store, or breaking into anyone's car or home. He had been riding his bicycle home after playing basketball. He had been shot and killed simply because of the NFL team jacket he had been wearing.

At that time, it was popular to wear a sports jacket with the logo of a professional sports team, such as the NBA Chicago Bulls or, as in this case, the NFL Oakland Raiders football team. The victim and his friend had left the Boys and Girls Club and were riding home on the dirt trail, when a car on Airline Drive skidded to a stop and one male jumped out with a gun in hand. The crook in this case ordered the boys to stop, and when the victim stopped, he was immediately shot several times. The crook then jerked the victim's Raiders jacket off of his dying body, reentered the car, and sped away. The other boy had never stopped his bicycle, but he had heard the gunshots and pedaled away as quickly as he could.

This brings me back to my original idea that Jesus is returning soon. One hallmark of the endtimes is the selfish, ungodly behavior of people. "This know also, that in the last days perilous times shall come. For men shall be lovers of their own selves, covetous, boasters, proud, blasphemers, disobedient to parents, unthankful, unholy, without natural affection, trucebreakers, false accusers, incontinent, fierce, despisers of those that are good" (2 Timothy 3:1–3 KJV). How many of the characteristics listed in these verses were evident in the murder of the young boy wearing the Raiders jacket?

When you consider the implications of these verses, you will begin to see that people's actions toward each other are good indicators of where mankind is, morally and spiritually. The phrase "disobedient to parents" indicates that you don't have to look any further than young people today to get an idea of how things are going. However, it isn't just the young people in our society who are going bad, but the adults as well.

Never in our history have we seen the coldness and lack of normal, natural human affection that we see in every evening news broadcast. Need I even mention the events that took place in Littleton, Colorado; Paduca, Kentucky; or Newtown, Connecticut? News broadcasts telling us about newborn babies found in trash cans and alley dumpsters are becoming so common that we barely take note, as we impatiently wait for the sports reporter to provide us with scores and details of the previous night's contests. Do the millions of unborn children losing their lives in our country ever cross your mind?

The abandonment of children has become so common that our country has had to come up with a safe-haven law, commonly referred to as the "Baby Moses Law," which makes it okay to abandon a child under sixty days of age at a designated infant emergency care provider, such as a fire station. Parents can legally abandon their babies at the proper location without fear of criminal prosecution. These are perilous times.

In Houston, several instances of abandonment of children older than sixty days have also been allowed. There is something gravely wrong with a society that is forced to legalize the abandonment of its youngest children in order to quell the abuse of murdering them.

"Human trafficking" is a phrase that few in our churches could define correctly if asked, and yet some 80 percent of Americans claim to be Christian.

Recently, in Houston, Texas, restaurant robberies and shootings have become so commonplace that we aren't even brought to tears or prayer over the violence. Yes, we live in perilous times.

Violent times have existed before today; we all know that. But to simply chalk the violence up to the increase in news coverage, or to write it off as inevitable, is to throw in the towel, to give up, to refuse to fight the good fight of faith.

Take every opportunity to share the love of Christ. What changes a society, I am convinced, isn't the winning of a political election or an argument. Rather, society is changed by the gospel, which is the power of God for salvation (Romans 1:16).

22

TAKING CHANCES

When I was a rookie, I saw a poster hanging in the evidence property room that had been made by one of the police unions. The poster showed a police car with the driver's-side door open. On the ground beside the patrol car was a police officer, facedown, his service revolver on the ground beside his body. The caption on the poster read, "You wouldn't risk your life for a million bucks. A police officer does it for a lot less." I have never forgotten that poster, and eventually I understood the reason why the union created it in the first place.

The year was 1989, and I was in something of a rut professionally. I suppose my current apathetic state could be attributed to all my experiences of the previous years: the harassment from "The Committee," endless paperwork, never-ending changes in policies and procedures, a few poor supervisors, and a small paycheck. I seriously lacked motivation. Perhaps "apathy" is not the best description of how I was feeling and behaving, but I had become lethargic in my work. I needed something to get me out of the rut I was in. Simply knowing Scripture was not energizing me.

I weighed my options. I could attempt a transfer out of patrol, but I knew that without knowing someone in an investigative division, I stood little chance of obtaining a transfer. I could transfer laterally within the patrol command to a new station, but I really liked Central Patrol and dismissed that idea quickly. When the opportunity presented itself, I took a position as a Field Training Instructor (FTI).

FTI school mostly consisted of boring instruction on how to fill out documentation paperwork and what constituted actual training. My final exam test score was tied for the highest in the class. It wasn't until I began to train my first rookie, though, that I became aware of just how deep a rut I had been in—and how poorly I had been doing my job as a patrolman. Becoming a trainer motivated me to improve my own performance and knowledge. Teaching rookie officers caused me to be a better police officer than I had ever been in the previous eight years. I learned more and became more proficient than I had ever been. All that I had originally desired to be—since that first day when I'd seen police officers up close in my parents' home—I was finally becoming.

When I trained rookie officers, one of the things I stressed most was safety. No matter what came our way during an eight-hour tour of duty, we were determined to go home in one piece at the end of each shift—and if not in one piece, at least to make it home alive. I faced a paradox, knowing that the only way to properly train these rookies was to intentionally expose them to the very dangers we were trying to survive. I felt that the best way to learn was to do something, not just talk about it.

A patrolman's job is dangerous enough without looking for trouble, and now things would become more dangerous for me. As a trainer, I not only had to run calls for service that were often high-risk, but I also had to train and watch out for the safety of the rookie officer who did not yet know what to do in high-stress situations.

Police officers working the streets talk about developing a sixth sense, a way to read people and situations that allows for correct spilt-second decision-making. This ability comes with experience, if it comes at all. If an officer is able to experience many different types of situations—and survive long enough to make mistakes and learn from them—then he or she can usually reach an above-average level of proficiency. In order for a rookie officer to gain these experiences, veteran officers have to take the time to teach them. Training rookies means taking extra chances with your life, and I am not sure that the extra pay is always worth the risk.

When I became a field trainer, I stepped up my game, so to speak, and began to lead the division in arrests and calls for service. Patrol work became enjoyable for me once again. It wasn't because I was a much better officer than others that made me so productive. It was my renewed sense of duty to adequately train the rookie officers assigned to me. The rookies I trained told the rookies who came after them to expect two things when I trained them: an increased dry-cleaning bill for their uniforms, and eight-hour shifts that lasted longer than eight hours. The way I looked at it, I was there to handle each call for service as if it was the only call I would handle that day. In other words, only 100-percent effort on training days was acceptable to me. The rut in which I had been was now gone. I was reinvigorated.

A few years later, after I had resigned from the Field Training Program, I did not slow down and return to my previously sluggish ways. As a result, I ended up with a few too many injuries, and my supervisors began to think I was accident-prone. For example, when I was a bike patrol officer in the central business district, a fellow officer observed me entering the station house with a suspect in custody. He looked at me and saw blood flowing steadily down the back of my right calf, which was turning my once-white sock red. He looked at me, and with genuine concern said, "Caronna, you need to slow down. You are getting into way too much stuff." *Stuff* wasn't the word he used, but I knew what he meant and appreciated his concern. That was only one of several injuries. Did I mention that I was on a first-name basis with the doctors and nurses at the old Heights Hospital?

One Thursday evening, my regular off day, I was again working the 655 overtime program that the mayor had put in place. This day was a six-hour overtime shift. As if I didn't get enough danger during my forty-hour patrol week, I had added an additional six or more hours to each week. The main goal of the program was the reduction of police response times. It was taking way too long for the police to respond to the scene after someone called them, because, frankly, there weren't many of us assigned to patrol at that time. The training academy had been shut down over a budget shortfall, and with veteran officers leaving in droves to retire, the department was becoming quite shorthanded.

Although we'd heard many speeches touting the patrolman as the backbone of the department, it was obvious to us patrolmen that those speeches were never backed up with the type of assistance we needed to do the job—namely, more patrolmen. Although the training academy had been restarted, it would take years to bring the numbers up. So the new mayor had run on a platform of increased safety by adding 655 more officers to the streets. Those 655 officers were not new; they were the same old tired officers working overtime.

This particular evening was slow. I had run a couple of calls, and now I slowly patrolled the neighborhoods in the lower Westheimer area. Driving north, away from Avondale Street, I glanced to my right and noticed a young man I recognized from a previous incident. Lamon Jackson was standing in an alleyway behind a small apartment complex.

I stepped on the brakes and backed the car up, although backing up to take a second look was not the safest thing to do. I reasoned in my mind that since I had dealt with Mr. Jackson before without serious problems, the potential for real danger was minimal. That was my mistake. My work ethic was great, but taking chances training rookies had bled over into my work as a one-man patrol unit. I knew that Lamon Jackson was not from the area, so I surmised that he must be up to no-good in that alley. I called out on my location and exited my car.

As I began to exit the patrol car, I saw Lamon remove something yellow from his pocket and attempt to nonchalantly toss it into the weeds nearby. He continued to stand there as if he belonged and nothing was wrong. That was his mistake.

Figuring that Lamon was in this Montrose neighborhood selling drugs, I immediately took him out of the alley, and after a search of his pockets, socks, and waistband for weapons, I placed him, without handcuffs, into the back of my patrol car. That was my second mistake. I quickly located the yellow item that Lamon had tossed into the grass and found it to be one of those little plastic eggs that come out of a gumball machine. However, it wasn't a gumball that I found inside the container, but two rocks of crack cocaine. After a field test of the rocks showed a positive result, I decided that Lamon was going to be charged with possession of a controlled substance, a felony.

I stood close to the patrol car and opened the door to the backseat as little as I possibly could. I told Lamon to turn his back toward me and place his hands behind his back and said that he was under arrest. Lamon was a teenager, about my height and not heavily built. My mind was telling me that there was a chance that he would try to escape the backseat of the car, so I kept a grip on the door frame in order to deny any attempt. Unfortunately for me, Lamon not only planned to escape from the patrol car, but he didn't hesitate in making the attempt. No sooner had I cracked open the car door than he kicked the door with all the might his skinny legs could muster—and the fight, as they say, was on.

I shoved Lamon back into the car as he had made it nearly halfway out. He continued to kick, and I tried my best to get a grip on him. I was now leaning forward into the backseat of the car. Lamon's kicks repeatedly connected with my right leg, knocking me off-balance. As I tried to gain control over Lamon in order to apply handcuffs, he bit me. Yes, Lamon, with all the teeth in his mouth, bit me on the right forearm and would not let go. It was like being in the jaws of a steel trap. I could not dislodge my arm from his mouth.

As I stated earlier, I had received a number of minor injuries in the line of duty prior to this, but none of those injuries compared to the pain I experienced from this human bite. It hurt a lot! I managed to key my radio microphone with my left hand and call for backup. However, the fight would not wait for the arrival of backup units. I had to do something fast. I still cannot figure out how I dislodged my arm from his mouth—or if he just let go—but I eventually pinned Lamon to the floorboard and applied the handcuffs, tightly.

The months that followed involved obtaining a court order to force Lamon to be tested for various diseases—and blood tests for me, to see if I had contracted any illness from him, which I had not. The bite from Lamon resulted in a painful infection that had to be treated.

The patrol officer's job is inherently dangerous, but few of us bargained for the injuries—such as a human bite—that we often received in the line of duty. Few people would volunteer for a job where the possibility of being killed is as high as it is in law enforcement. Each year, law enforcement tends to rank in the lower top ten of the deadliest jobs in America. There is not enough pay for the work, but the pay isn't why we do it.

Job danger rankings usually fail to report that the suicide rate among law enforcement officers is regularly double that of the national average. The additional stress placed on law enforcement officers by the community they serve is often indescribable. The community holds officers to a very high standard, as well it should. Few in the community, however, have any real understanding of just what the job involves, and those who do understand seldom want the job themselves.

There is great responsibility that comes with the badge, and nearly every officer I had the honor of serving with took that responsibility very seriously. However, the pressure of life-and-death, split-second decision-making, coupled with often unfair news media coverage of an incident, pushes the pressure level too high for many officers. A look at the negative comments made toward police officers by people on social media is revealing. It is shocking to some people, including some police officers, that more police officers die at their own hands each year than are killed in the line of duty.

Let me ask you something. When was the last time you initiated a positive conversation with a law enforcement officer? Have you considered Romans 13:1–7?

> "Every person is to be in subjection to the governing authorities. For there is no authority except from God, and those which exist are established by God. Therefore whoever resists

authority has opposed the ordinance of God; and they who have opposed will receive condemnation upon themselves. For rulers are not a cause of fear for good behavior, but for evil. Do you want to have no fear of authority? Do what is good and you will have praise from the same; for it is a minister of God to you for good. But if you do what is evil, be afraid; for it does not bear the sword for nothing; for it is a minister of God, an avenger who brings wrath on the one who practices evil. Therefore it is necessary to be in subjection, not only because of wrath, but also for conscience' sake. For because of this you also pay taxes, for *rulers* are servants of God, devoting themselves to this very thing. Render to all what is due them: tax to whom tax *is due;* custom to whom custom; fear to whom fear; honor to whom honor."

Please read those verses slowly and carefully, and realize that law enforcement officers, as agents of the government in your area, have an awesome responsibility given to them by God. Please encourage your local law enforcement officers. Pray for them, invite them to your church and your home, and deliver baked goodies to the local police station. Their job is incredibly stressful and dangerous, and kind deeds go a long way toward bridging gaps between law enforcement and the community they serve.

Officers, whether or not you choose to acknowledge God in your life, understand that your job is more than a way to pay your bills. You are functioning as a part of God's plan, whether you realize it or not.

I remember having been asked a few times over the years how a Christian could work as a police officer. I believe that the question is based on a misunderstanding of God's plan for governing authorities and the punishment of lawbreakers. Would you prefer that unbelievers patrol your streets?

I saw my work as a calling from God, and since Romans 13 clearly tells us that God instituted the governing authorities, I think the better question might be: how can we encourage more Christians to enter the law enforcement profession?

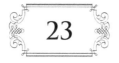

23

Wrap-Up

"Whatever you do, do your work heartily, as for the Lord rather than for men, knowing that from the Lord you will receive the reward of the inheritance. It is the Lord Christ whom you serve" (Colossians 3:23–24).

When I transferred into the Central Patrol Division, I received a warning from several fellow officers. They warned me not to park a patrol car anywhere near the main complex that wasn't an actual, marked parking space for police vehicles. They said that there was an officer who would write a parking ticket and even tow the patrol car away, resulting in much grief and letter-writing to explain why the car had been parked illegally. To them, it was unthinkable for an officer to write a parking ticket to a fellow officer. They felt that the police station property was there for their exclusive use. Since parking was at a premium around the various buildings of what was then the main police station, they believed that they should be able to park their cars anywhere they wanted, provided they were there for official police business. They also had some choice words and names for the officer who wrote the parking tickets—names that will not be printed here. You get the picture.

I listened to their complaints, and initially I felt that their arguments had merit. We were conducting the dangerous business of police work, and when we needed to book a prisoner into the jail, we couldn't find a parking space close by. How could any officer have the nerve to write me a parking ticket and place it on the windshield of my marked police car? He should get out there and be a real policeman like me and catch real crooks, right?

The complaints continued, until the day someone found that particular officer dead in his police car at the main gas pumps. This served as a reminder to me from the Lord. I had apparently forgotten my own experiences and calling from God. In previous years, I had taken my calling seriously enough to go against the flow and cross the thin blue line, facing several years of grief and problems because I had sought to please God rather than my coworkers. Hadn't I determined that there existed a higher calling than the call to popularity and peer approval?

Yes, I had. Why, then, had I been looking down my nose at this officer, who was simply doing the job assigned to him to the best of his abilities? In my heart, I had become a hypocrite. The man had apparently died from a heart attack while sitting in his patrol car at the gas pumps. He had died alone, his tour of duty ended. What I heard from other officers about his passing must have grieved God's heart. It did mine, and I needed to repent of my hardened heart.

That officer had been disliked by many because of the way he worked. I do not know why he had been assigned this duty, but he showed no partiality. He simply did the job assigned to him. Although he was not popular, he was respected—and perhaps feared just a little bit. His supervisors also knew that they could count on him to do a thankless job.

My purpose in writing this book is twofold. On the one hand, I hope that you Christians in law enforcement might be encouraged and motivated to do the very best that can be done. Yours is often a thankless job. Remember to do your duties as to the Lord, from whom your reward comes. Be steadfast, be honest, show respect to all people, and try to begin each encounter with coworkers or the public in a God-honoring way. Do not compromise your morals or your ethics. Be a bold witness for Christ, without becoming an obnoxious jerk. Please, let your light shine. Other believing officers need someone to show them the way. How much easier it would have been for me if the few officers who professed Christ had helped me through those difficult times when I struggled. There should be no secret agents for Christ.

On the other hand, if you are not a Christian, or you are unsure about all the religious statements and Bible verses found in this book, I want to say something to you. Although you and I will not fully understand all of the tragedies and sorrows of this life, there is a God who created the world, and He loves you. The God of the universe will one day put an end to all of the injustice we see around us. Until that time, for as long as you have breath, please understand that God desires to have an intimate relationship with you.

If you will, by faith, understand that you are separated from God's love because of your sins, and believe that Jesus Christ paid your penalty with His own life when He died in your place, was buried, and rose from the dead three days later—you can be saved. By faith, surrender your life to Him. Seek His forgiveness, and allow Him to be in charge of your life from this day forward.

Read these words from the apostle Paul: "That if you confess with your mouth Jesus as Lord, and believe in your heart that God raised Him from the dead, you will be saved; for with the heart a person believes, resulting in righteousness, and with the mouth he confesses, resulting in salvation" (Romans 10:9–10).

After that, take God with you on patrol, wherever He may lead you.

Lightning Source UK Ltd.
Milton Keynes UK
UKHW010758250821
389434UK00001B/29